C0 1 66

GW00707351

THE TUMBLER

ASSA (Košice) - AUSCHWITZ - SWEDEN - ISRAEL

THE TUMBLER

KASSA (Košice) - AUSCHWITZ - SWEDEN - ISRAEL

A TRUE STORY

Deported with his family to Auschwitz Nazi death camp when he was only 16 years old

Azriel Feuerstein

First Edition
Published in Great Britain
by Mirage Publishing 2007

Text Copyright © Azriel Feuerstein 2007

First published in paperback 2007

No part of this publication may be reproduced,
stored in a retrieval system or transmitted in any
form or by any means without first seeking
the written authority from the publisher.
The purchase or possession of this book
In any form deems acceptance
of the conditions.

A CIP catalogue record for this book
Is available from the British Library.

ISBN 978-1-90257-832-3

Mirage Publishing
PO Box 161
Gateshead
NE8 4WW
Great Britain

Printed and bound in Great Britain by

Forward Press
Remus House, Coltsfoot Drive, Woodston,
Peterborough, PE2 9JX

Cover designed by Raanan Beeri
Cover © Raanan Beeri

Papers used in the production of this book are recycled,
thus reducing environmental depletion.

For my wife Annika, with thankfulness and love

Durham County Council Libraries, Learning and Culture	
C0 1 66 14997 BB	
Askews	
940.5315296	

Contents

PART I

1

Fröken Ulle

Gyurika!!! The desperate cry, the unforgettable nightmare. But no! What awoke me from the slumber over my books was the sound of Fröken[1] Ulle Olofson's somewhat hesitant knocking. This sound was slightly different now, because of the echo in the boarding school's empty corridors.

'God Dag, Fröken Ulle,' I greeted her, as usual. I was truly glad about her not so unexpected visit. It was the Easter holidays, and the cloudy, overcast sky, so typical of Sweden at that time of year, and the boarding school's empty rooms, made me moody and sad.

'Hej, Yeorj,' answered Fröken Ulle, with her friendly smile. 'How about some coffee and cookies?'

I am afraid that my answer was perhaps too enthusiastic, beyond the customary good manners. It had been six months since I had left the sanatorium and the rest home and, although I trained myself to return to civilized table manners, I still did not refuse food, especially cookies.

Fröken Ulle was then, in 1946, about fifty years old which, in the eyes of an eighteen year old, was a very old age indeed. Tall and slim, her hair was still blonde and pulled back. Her lips were thin, with wrinkles in the corners of her mouth that told of pain and disappointments, and her womanly curves were severely disciplined by her overly modest clothing. Only the softness in her blue eyes told of her good heartedness and generosity. Her manner of speech was purposeful, dry and ceremonial in the

---

[1] Fröken translates in to English as the female title of Miss.

THE TUMBLER

courteous and somewhat archaic manner as was then accepted in Sweden. Only an occasional gleam of mischievousness in her eyes made me suspect that she may even have a spark of humour, but she was very Swedish, perhaps my suspicions were unfounded.

Fröken Ulle was responsible for the cleaning of the students' rooms in Folkshögskolan Fjällhögen and ruled with an iron fist over the two chambermaids, Britta and Inga. She inspected the rooms after the cleaning and always found something additional to wipe. A yellow dust cloth and a feather duster were part of her uniform and I seldom saw her without them. I think that she was somewhat shy and preferred, so I was told, to drink her afternoon tea alone, before I invaded her life.

Folkshögskolan, in literal translation meaning 'popular high schools', were then in the hands of big organisations, such as trade unions or churches, and they served as schools for their activists who learned at home but wanted to review the material before the graduation examinations, and also indoctrinated them in their ideology during a six-month term.

Our school, Fjällhögen, was situated in a small village, not far from Gotheburg, an important seaport and the second largest city in Sweden. Its imposing building stood in a big park with a number of huge oaks and was surrounded by well-tended lawns. It looked like a palace and its wings served as rooms for the students and the personnel. I came there mainly to improve my Swedish and was the only non-Scandinavian in a school where the vast majority were Swedish, with some Norwegians, Danes and Finns thrown in.

I arrived in the afternoon and went down to the small dining room for five o'clock tea or, in my case, coffee. I sat down, unwittingly, in Fröken Ulle's regular place. Nobody warned me about it, partly because of the usual Swedish good manners and reticence, but also through compassion and strangeness mixed with curiosity. As I learned later, the principal of the school, Dr Yustus, let it discreetly be known that a survivor of the Concentration Camps, a youth from Czechoslovakia who within a

10

few months had recovered and learned Swedish, had come to the school as a student, and that 'Yeory had to be treated with care and sympathy'.

Fröken Ulle came in, looked around and sat down on the other side of the table.

'My name is Fröken Ulle,' she said, shaking my hand. 'May I sit down?'

'Var so god, Fröken Ulle,' I replied, standing up, demonstrating both my Swedish and my manners. 'I'll be honoured and glad. My name is Yeory.'

'Ya-ha,' said Fröken Ulle, using the Jolly-Joker of her language that is accompanied by a strong intake of breath, a word that is an unending source of amusement to all who are unaware of the beauties of the Swedish language, the meaning of which varies between *yes, no, perhaps, really*, all according to the tone, situation and context.

'How come you have a Swedish name?' she asked.

I replied, 'The name "Yeory" is only the Swedish version of the English George, and that is a translation of Gyuri, my name in Hungarian. Here I should mention that in Swedish they write my name Georg, but pronounce it as Yeory.'

'Gyu…' Fröken Ulle tried to accustom her lips to the strange, foreign tones. 'I shall continue to call you Yeory, if you don't mind, but why do you have a Hungarian name? You are from Czechoslovakia, aren't you?'

Now, go and try to explain it to her, a daughter of a lucky, homogenous land, without minorities, without problems with its neighbours; a country whose entire population is Swedish, nearly all tall, blond(e), with blue eyes, whose girls have a peach-like complexion because of the climate. Try to explain to her the mish-mash of languages, peoples and religions in Eastern Europe and Czechoslovakia, where Hungarians, Slovaks, Czechs and Germans live together, with different languages, heritages, cultures and religions, without too much love for each other and that the only thing they have in common is the deep mistrust or hate against their Jewish neighbours.

THE TUMBLER

The mother tongue of my family, like that of most Jews in my hometown, Kosice, was Hungarian. Kosice was part of Austro-Hungary until the end of the First World War in 1918, was part of Czechoslovakia from 1918 until 1938, part of Hungary from 1938 until the end of the Second World War in 1945 and from then on, Czechoslovakia again.

I went to a second language and I learned the four years of elementary school in Slovak because that was then the language of the land. In 1938, Kosice became part of Hungary.

My name in German is Georg, in Czech Jiri, in Slovak Juraj and in Hungarian Gyuri. I even had a name in Hebrew, Azriel Yaakov, a name that was used in the synagogue only when I was called to the Torah. Now, try to explain that, and what is more, do it in Swedish, to Fröken Ulle. I was sorry for us both.

She did not wait for an answer. She blushed lightly. It was a personal question, which really was not done, and she changed the subject. 'How do you feel in Sweden?' she asked.

I spoke about the weather (it will clear up), about the housemother (pedantic, but nice), about Dr Yustus, the headmaster (a very special person), and all after an introductory visit of about five minutes. These remained more or less the subjects of our conversations at all our subsequent meetings at five o'clock teas for the rest of the term, with one exception.

The next day after our initial meeting, she arrived before me and sat down in her accustomed place. She was without her apron. She wore a blue blouse and skirt and I saw that, despite her thinness, her breasts were round and full. I think that she was glad to see me and I too was happy for her company.

I was alone in a foreign land, among unknown people, and the presence of an elderly, likeable and nice woman answered in me a deeply felt need, a strange hope that filled a void, which I was unaware of. She never forgot to compliment me for my progress in Swedish, instructed me in the mysteries of handing in and collecting the laundry and always asked whether I needed an additional pillow or cover.

2

The Way to Sweden

I was very lonely in those days. In fact, I had been very lonely ever since my mother's desperate cry at the railway station in Auschwitz on 17 May 1944.

This period in Sweden was like waking up after a dangerous operation. You begin to be aware of the ache and make an inventory: what remains and what they have cut away. You are in shock and do not feel any real pain yet, but you know that it will hurt very, very much.

I was liberated from the Bergen-Belsen Concentration Camp on 15 April 1945, two days before my seventeenth birthday. To tell the truth, it was not I who was liberated, but somebody else who bore my name. That man knew his name, but not much more. There were cloudy memories bubbling up in what remained of his brain, unconnected facts from his past, strange feelings of pain and fear and the deeply engraved knowledge in his whole being that he is hungry. This creature tottered unsafely on his spindle-legs, pronouncing his name with difficulty. His being was full of one word, one feeling: hunger, and of one longing only: food. He was really not I, but to make things simpler I am going to speak about him in the first person singular.

How much I weighed then, I do not know, but after two months in an English military hospital, I weighed 28 kg. At the end of the Second World War Sweden was among the very few countries in Europe that were neutral and did not suffer any damage from the war and it offered relief and rehabilitation for thousands of former Concentration Camp prisoners. That is how I came to Lübeck, a Swedish disinfection camp in Germany.

THE TUMBLER

I got there on a stretcher of course, but was able to walk around a bit. I had a small paper bag and in it a piece of bread, a dirty shirt and pants that were too big for me – everything was too big for me then (but believe me, not now) - a blue and grey Concentration Camp cap, a worn out leather belt that I used in Bergen-Belsen for dragging corpses and a torn book in Hungarian. In Lübeck I had to take part in a procedure which at that time was carried out all over Europe.

1) We had to strip
2) All our hair was shorn off
3) We were powdered with DDT (a synthetic pesticide)

To this routine the Swedes added another procedure: they took everything you had and burned it to prevent, as far as possible, the spreading of infections and lice. They took everything from the others, but not from me. I let them take the clothes, even the bread, but not the cap, the belt and the book. After much persuasion, I let them take the book. But the cap and belt – no way!

'If so, you can't come into Sweden.'

'So I won't.'

'OK, you will get them back after the disinfection.'

But I was too experienced to believe in promises and I followed my precious possessions, naked as I was, from station to station.

They disinfected them, they washed them, they cooked them for two hours and I stayed and waited. At last, I got them back, sealed in a white paper bag and they have been with me to this very day. So I came to Sweden, like the others, in a white paper hospital shirt but, unlike the others, with a *paper bag too*.

The provisional hospital-quarantine was in Malmö, an important port in Southern Sweden, situated in a medieval castle that was surrounded by a moat. We stayed there for a couple of weeks for medical examinations and were sorted out for future destinations.

Azriel Feuerstein

It was a paper hospital. The mattresses, the bed sheets, the pillows, the covers, the shirts and pants of both the patients and the personnel, were made of paper to be burned after we left. We, the patients, were all infected with various diseases that had been unknown in Europe for years and, of course, we were all clinically underfed.

After the medical examination it was found that I had pleurisy (water in the lungs), chronic itching and recurring diarrhea, which was no wonder because we all ate like pigs. They sent me to a hospital for a month and after that to a rest home, Olofsfors, near Avesta, a small town in the north. Before I write about my life in Sweden, I have to briefly explain about that man, that boy, who survived.

Until March 1944, one month before my sixteenth birthday, I was the only child of well-off parents, pampered and somewhat plump. Plump? Let us say fat. I was lucky because, as the 'poet' of my age group, I was not ridiculed as many fat boys are and the nicknames were mingled with respect and liking of a sort, but they hurt nonetheless. I had many friends and was part of the group since I was a good swimmer and a goalkeeper in football games.

As the youngest grandchild in both my father's and my mother's family, I was surrounded by love. I was smart for my age and my witty sayings made their rounds among the aunts. I was a 'high-school student' and they were proud of me.

Less than two months later, after the German occupation on 17 May 1944, I found myself in Auschwitz, Häftling number 37278, an orphan and alone in the world, without yet being aware of the fact.

When I arrived in Auschwitz, I was fat and I remembered a Slovak saying: 'Until the fat man grows thin, the thin one dies'. What saved me for a time from the pangs of hunger was not my being fat, but the fact that fat people are ashamed to talk about hunger and cannot admit even to themselves that they are thinking about food. That fact helped me to overcome my hunger for a few weeks when all around me were complaining about being hungry, despite the fact that we were still supposed to get 1600 calories daily for fourteen hours of hard labour. One day, after some weeks, I put my hand on my belly and for the first time felt my bowels moving under the muscles. I felt a kind of vulnerability and defencelessness in the absence of the hated, but protecting, layers of fat, and only then did I permit myself to be aware of the persistent feeling of hunger. From that day on, the hunger grew and permeated every thought and feeling. The fear of death made you forget the hunger for a time, as did the feeling of comradeship when you shared your piece of bread with a friend, but gradually hunger overcame it all.

Everyone has seen the pictures of the liberation of the concentration camps: the moving skeletons, those skull-like faces, and the protruding hipbones. These are only the outward signs. After the hungry body finishes eating away the stored fat, after it devours the muscles, after the skin dries out and becomes like the scales of a fish, the body begins to eat away the brain. It constricts the memory, the pride, the feelings, and leaves behind a dark emptiness that defies description. The man is still breathing but he does not exist. All that remains is the hunger.

Eventually, the skeleton falls down and does not breathe any more. Not that anybody cares: other skeletons surround him. The only sign that he is dead is the long line of lice making their way to his loin. Why? Who knows? Perhaps that part of the body remains warm longest.

Sometimes, something happens, a miracle or liberation, and he gets food. The feeling of hunger does not stop when the belly is full. He eats, but he is still hungry. He is unable to eat any more, but he still feels empty. He begins to be aware that he can't be hungry any more, but he still fears being hungry.

Then, suddenly, something begins to move. His skin, which was like the scales of a fish, peels off. Like a snake, he sheds his skin. He does not cry at any loud or unexpected noise anymore. In the darkness of his brain, some lights twinkle: recollections, faces that he once loved, stubs of feelings and pain, memories of his family. Half-forgotten fragments of poems and melodies surface and disappear. He knows that he is on his way back to life, he wishes it and yet at the same time he is afraid of what he will find there: being alone. Behind everything lurks the threatening shadow of hunger. He is undernourished, but recovering.

I became aware of these changes after a few weeks in the hospital in Malmö and to a greater extent in the sanatorium at Olofsfors, in North Sweden. We arrived there in November of 1945. There was already heavy snow, but now I did not tremble from cold anymore. I began to remember poems, Hungarian and Slovakian folksongs and to sing them with great gusto and enjoyment. I still do it today. I have to say that the enjoyment is only mine because all my listeners maintain, brazenly and without shame, that I sing terribly. I began to seek books. I was, and still am, an omnivorous reader. I read anything and everything that I can lay my hands on: books, newspapers, advertisements, labels on jars and bottles – everything. If it is in a language I know, very well. If it is in a language I don't know, I read it anyway. That is the way I learn new languages.

There were very few books in Hungarian or Slovakian, so I began to read German. I had a German nurse until I was four years old and went to a German kindergarten. In high school we read German for three years as a foreign language, so I had some knowledge of it. I saw that German and Swedish are very much alike if you ignore the peculiar pronunciation of Swedish, and so I began to read Swedish books as well. At that time the doctors decided that I had recovered enough, and they sent me to a transit camp near Göteborg as a last stage before going 'home' or going to work in Sweden.

Göteborg is an ancient city and a very important port in Sweden; nice, peaceful and very clean, with many canals and extensive green public parks and friendly, helpful people. I was very lucky with the Swedes of both sexes as I met only good people. I know that the Swedes are like other human beings, and it is only reasonable to suppose that among them there were good and better, bad and worse people, but the last ones I did not meet. Until I came to this transit camp, I had been in hospitals and

17

sanatoriums and in all those places I had met volunteers, who took upon themselves a very hard and even dangerous work. They took care of people who had undergone terrible experiences, people who had survived in inhuman surroundings and who, in order to survive, had to submerge in this world, people with contagious diseases that were long forgotten in the modern world, people who woke up screaming in the night from unspeakable nightmares. People who had got used to the fact that a moment of weakness meant certain death. Children who had got used to taking everything that did, and did not belong to them, who had got used to sleeping next to corpses. They not only had to be healed, they had to be returned to human society.

I spent only one year in this inhuman world. I arrived there at the age of sixteen, an age when I already knew about human values, yet not once did I recoil from these children who had grown up in camps and who had got used to tramping on everything that stood in their way. In the Swedish staff, the doctors, the nurses and others, I did not see this instinctive revolt. There I found infinite patience, caressing hands, soothing words and warm feelings. I was sure that these people, being volunteers, were different and better than ordinary people. But even when I got out of this closed milieu and met the men on the street, in school, at work, I found the Swedes nearly always ready to help and always friendly (except the bureaucrats, who are the same everywhere) despite the fact that they are very reticent by nature. I was lucky to find all this in the transit camp in Göteborg.

This camp consisted of some fifteen Swedish barracks, each with five rooms with four people. Of these fifteen barracks, only one was for men. The rest were for women, which is an interesting ratio that boosts your self-esteem if you are a teenage boy.

Within a short period of time I became very friendly with the female secretary of the camp, Kerstin. She was a beautiful, slender woman in her forties. She was very impressed by my fluent German, even more so when I began to read Swedish, and would even stammer a few words. She was well read and, like me, loved literature, so we always had something to talk about. After a short time she offered me the position of librarian to put in order and catalogue the many books in foreign languages that people sent to the camp for the survivors. The library was located in a small barrack between the office and the storeroom. It consisted of a big room with a set of shelves for the books, a small, well-lit office, a small kitchen and a private toilet and bathroom! Kerstin even agreed that I move into the library with my bed and all my possessions. I was very happy with my newfound privacy after having lived in such confines with so many people for such a long time.

This privacy enhanced my position in the camp and certainly improved my social life. It brought me many new friends who were eager to explore the books with their girlfriends in the evenings. All this came to an abrupt end when I found myself wandering about too much in the fresh air, and when I had on one occasion lent the key to my Czech friend, Milan (whose private parts had become almost legendary around the camp). I came home to find my towel covered with a strange, sticky fluid. I changed the lock of the barrack and, I am sorry to say, lost many friends.

I continued to enjoy my private residence, my work, and my prestigious position as librarian, thereby belonging to the social and intellectual elite of the camp. After a couple of months, when I could read Swedish without any difficulty and my casual conversations with Kerstin had grown into a real and deep friendship, she took me with her to the social circles she used to visit: pale pink circles of world-savers and literary fringes of writers and poets. She managed to get me a scholarship for Folkshögskolan Fjällhögen, and that is how I came to meet Fröken Ulle.

3

The Notebook

I tried not to sleep in the afternoon, when the nightmares used to reoccur. Luckily, Fröken Ulle's knocking on my door saved me.
'Hey, Yeory, how are you?'
'Thank you, Fröken Ulle, I am OK. And how are you?'
'Don't we miss May-Britt?'
May-Britt! What does she know about May-Britt? I thought to myself. May-Britt was my age, not very pretty, with all her womanly attributes at great, but not excessive, abundance. She was not taller than me, short for a Swede, calm, calming and very curious, not about my experiences in the concentration camps, but just about me being so foreign, so not Swedish.

She came from a small village in North Sweden and it was her first time away from the home she loved and talked much about. I understood that in her village even a visit by somebody from the nearby township was something to talk about.

And now, she, little May-Britt was far away from home, among many kinds of people, and here was a really exotic boy from a far away land whose very name was even hard to pronounce. I thought to myself that I would be a very interesting topic of conversation with her girlfriends in the long, snowy nights. I had to believe that it was my personality that interested her because the calmness, that so attracted me, did not even leave her in situations, where calmness is not the most flattering response. It was she who, during our walks in the park, led me to the bushes near the little lake behind the school building and gave me all the necessary technical help and advice with buttons and hooks and only seldom asked 'Again?' with sweet patience.

THE TUMBLER

'Your company gives me solace,' I answered gallantly to Fröken Ulle.

'Ya-ha?!' (Meaning 'really'.) 'My company and the cookies, no doubt?' Fröken Ulle, a sense of humour? She continued, 'I heard that you got pictures from home.'

She must have heard it from Irmgård, the postmistress. The old maids' mafia worked without faults and speedily. The package was on the table: a big brown envelope, torn only at one corner. I had only read the letter since I had no courage to look at the pictures yet.

'What! You haven't opened the package yet? When I get a letter, I must open it in the post office,' replied Fröken Ulle.

'No, I did not have the courage to look into the eyes of so many dead people,' I responded,

I explained to Fröken Ulle that the package was the most precious gift I ever hoped to get. In it were the pictures of my family, I was sure were lost forever.

'I am so very happy for you. How did it happen?' asked Fröken Ulle.

'Margit the saleslady from my father's store sent it. She risked being arrested for it. Some days after we were deported she went to our house and found the pictures in the garbage can and collected them, in spite of the neighbours calling her a whore of the Jews. What is more, she saved them for more than two years, until she got my address. I never shall be able to thank her for it.'

'But why didn't you open it yet?'

'I only read the letter. I am afraid to look at the pictures alone. I hoped to look at them with you. By the way, you asked me about my life at home and in the Concentration Camps. If you are interested, here is this notebook, it contains all.'

Fröken Ulle turned away, her eyes were red.

'Of course, I'll read it, and I am honoured that you want to see the pictures together. We'll do it the next time. Now I must really run, because the headmaster wants to see me.'

4

Family and Hometown

I was born on St George's Day on 17 April 1928, at three o'clock in the morning in Košice, or 'Kassa' in Hungarian, according to my mother. The name on my birth certificate is Juraj Feuerstein, but my first name in Czech is Jiri, or George in English, or Georg in German and Swedish. Everybody called me Gyuri, my first name in Hungarian, pronounced something like Djuri, but don't try to pronounce it. All these are no more than the variations of the name of the saint who fought the dragon and on whose day I was born. My name in Hebrew is Azriel Yaakov, after my maternal grandfather, but this name was used in religious ceremonies only.

The name Azriel Yaakov is an ancient one in my mother's family and, according to the family tale, the first Azriel Yaakov Altmann was a martyr of a small pogrom in his native Poland in 1650. His widow fled to Germany with her two sons and both the firstborns of her two sons were named after the martyr Azriel Yaakov. Since then the name has become a tradition, in every second generation, for the firstborn of both sons and daughters. My grandfather, Azriel Yaakov (or Izidor by his secular name), was born in 1850 in Prešov, or Eperjes in Hungarian. His education, as for most of his contemporaries, was strictly religious but he completed it by secular reading in German and Hungarian. In his time there was a bitter struggle between orthodoxy, the more liberal neology and the status quo in which my grandfather took the side of the orthodoxy and, as a leader of the Jewish community, he was the prime mover in keeping the 'kehila' (community) orthodox. In spite of this, he was an ardent

Zionist, one of the founders of the religious Zionist organisation 'Mizrachi' in Slovakia and even one of its delegates in the Zionist Congress in Geneva.

On top of his public activities, he was also a very successful businessman. He expanded his tavern on Main Street to a restaurant and small hotel and bought a big parcel of land between Main Street and its parallel. This became the family's headquarters. Azriel Yaakov and his wife, Frumett, born Gutman, had six daughters and three sons. The firstborn boy of each one of these children got their grandfather's name. He died in 1910 at the age of sixty and, two weeks after his death, the biggest Jewish newspaper in the German language in Budapest, the *Jüdische Allgemeine Rundschau* published his obituary, which was carefully preserved by every one in the family.

His wife, Frumett Altmann, born Gutmann, also had, as per tradition, a family tree of even deeper roots to be proud of. Her mother was Esther Hanna Gobiner and her great-grandfather was Avraham Aveli Gobiner, the author of the book *Magen Avraham*, was the descendant of Rabbi Shimon Luria (Hamaharshal). The genealogy continues through Yoselman, the biggest intercessor in the sixteenth century in Germany, who was called the king of the Jews, through Rashi, the commentator of the Talmud and Rabbi Napcha of Talmudic fame, who, as everyone knows, is a direct descendant of King David. Q.E.D. At this point I used to interrupt the teller of the tale, who told it with awesome reverence in his eyes, and make him very angry by telling him that the deeper we descend to the roots of the family tree, the nearer we get to the monkey. However, it is clearly more prestigious to find King David at the roots of your family tree than to rummage around its drying branches for some eventual jailbirds or beggars. The fact is that even I used to recount this nice legend, as I remain the only one who survived to tell it.

On my father's side, the genealogy is much shorter but no less honourable. As the family tradition has it, at the end of the eighteenth century, the first Feuerstein Lajos was among the first ten Jews who were allowed to build a two-storey house in our city, Kassa, but I could not find any documentation about it. The first document I found was of my great-grandfather, Feuerstein Mayer, who was the chief contractor of the first railroad that went through our hometown, the Kassa-Oberberg. He lived in a splendid two-storey house and got rich enough to send his son, my grandfather, to an officers' school and buy him into one of the finest regiments of Austro-Hungary as a lieutenant. My grandfather, Feuerstein Lajos, who was born in 1866, served no more than six or seven years. He took part in punishing expeditions in Bosnia and felt so much at home in the squandering atmosphere of his fellow officers, who were from the gentry and rich land-owner families, that until his discharge he succeeded in 'liberating' his father from most of his money. He married Adel Bottenstein, who came from a respectable but not prosperous family, and with her dowry bought a tavern in one of the villages near Kassa. They had two girls and four boys and, though not exactly poor, lived much below the prosperous circumstances of their grandfather until my father got enough money to help them. From this whole family I am the only one who survived the Holocaust, as the Nazis murdered all the others. In the course of my tale I shall tell you about some of them, and at the end of the book I shall recount all their names as I remember them.

Before I talk about my small nuclear family, my mother, my father and myself, I have to say a few words about my hometown, Kassa or Košice in Slovakian. Kassa was a county seat in the era of Austro-Hungary until 1918, the capital of East-Slovakia under the name of Kosice in Czechoslovakia until 1938, Kassa again under the Hungarians until 1945 and part of Czechoslovakia and later Slovakia after the end of World War II as Košice again. I shall call it mostly Kassa in order not to confuse the reader.

As an old and important city, its official buildings, such as the courts of law, the city hall, the military headquarters and the banks, were all built in the style of the Austro-Hungarian Empire to last for centuries and, above all, the cathedral known as the Dome, the pride of the city and the central part of every picture postcard. The Dome was the biggest, but not the only, church. There were many places of worship of every Christian and Jewish denomination. There was the big and magnificent theatre building in the middle of a big park that divided Main Street, where every theatre from Budapest played two or three weeks after the premiere in the capital. Kassa was an important railway centre, with a big railway station and an extensive park, the 'Liget', in front of it. At its centre there was an ornate iron pavilion where, on summer Sundays, military orchestras gave concerts that attracted a big crowd of listeners, the paying ones in chairs, and the rest standing. In the park there was also a tennis court that in the winter doubled as a skating rink, an important gathering place for the youth of 'better circles'. At the other side of the park, with its ancient chestnut trees and open spaces of well-tended grass, was the Lido with two swimming pools, the meeting place of the same better circles in the summer.

Before nostalgia overcomes us, we had better remember that, at the far end of this pleasant park, through that ancient railway station, from mid-May 1944, within forty-one days, three hundred and ninety-five thousand Hungarian Jews, among them thirteen thousand from Kassa and the villages around it, were deported to the slaughterhouse in Auschwitz.

Main Street was more than fifty metres wide and cobble stoned, with the Theatre in its middle. Parks with sculptures, little ornamental fountains and a big fountain that was illuminated in the evenings in all the colours of the rainbow – well, red, blue, green and white - surrounded it. It was the only coloured fountain in Slovakia, until the people in Bratislava got jealous and built another one but, as reliable people (from Kassa) said 'ours was much more impressive'. There was another park, some two hundred metres long, and at its end there was a pedestal with a different statue in every regime, but the real Košicans called it the statue of Stefanik. On both sides of this long green island there were roads and wide sidewalks with stores and cafés, whose chairs occupied part of the sidewalks and old ladies selling flowers in summer and hot chestnuts in winter. At the crossroads there were electric lights, but along the sidewalks there were gaslights on high and decorative iron poles. Every evening before nightfall, an elderly man with a long pole walked by the gas lamps and ignited the gas.

Every Sunday an important ceremony took place on Main Street, or more exactly on its right side, between the Dome in the South and the military headquarters in the North: the promenade or 'Korzo'. The ceremony began approximately at ten o'clock, after the prayer in the churches, but non-prayers and Jews took part in it too. Married couples, engaged ones with parents not too far behind them, daring couples on their own (who were talked about behind their backs), teenagers, boys and girls in separate groups, everyone in their Sunday best walked up and down, greeting acquaintances, meeting and separating, with the groups of girls snickering in the most embarrassing way. At one o'clock the 'Korzo' of the 'better people' was over, but for some days it remained a most interesting topic of conversation: who looked at whom, how long, and why.

The 'Korzo' of the domestic maids was on the other side of the street and commenced at four o'clock in the afternoon. That was the time when they got their weekly leave, usually until nine o'clock in the evening. At the same time, the soldiers of the neighbouring barracks got their weekly leave too, so the two groups met on the 'Korzo', paired off and went to the big park, the 'Liget', where there was more privacy for conversations and other intimate activities.

In the middle of Main Street there was a tramway line. Its end station was in 'Csermely', some three kilometres outside of town, at the beginning of the extensive forests where those who chose to walk the nature trails instead of the 'Korzo' got off in the early hours of Sunday mornings.

Around Kassa there were big forests through which you could walk until you reached Poland and, some said, even to the Ural. Near every footpath there was a brook or creek, with clear, cold water and small springs. The forest was full of all kinds of good things in all seasons if you only knew where to look. There were all kinds of fragrant wild flowers, and mushrooms of every kind which we learned to recognise; fragrant, small, wild strawberries, that you could buy for a pittance in the markets, but tasted much better if you plucked them yourself; raspberries, plums, wild apples and even hazelnuts if you knew their secret places. But chiefly you took pleasure in walking around in the fresh air of the forest with the intention of reaching the destination of the day: the Banko, the Ottilia, where there were roughly hewn tables and benches where you could eat what you brought from home or ordered from the kiosks there.

When I came to Sweden, and, after time, became a man again, I was very homesick for my town. I dreamed about the Dome, about Main Street and the Liget, about grandma's house and garden. Return there for good, I did not want (I had enough sense for that), but I longed very much to see Kassa again. At the first opportunity when I had enough money saved for the trip, I returned for a month. The first time I walked down Main Street, I saw that I was not in the town that I loved and dreamed about. Unknown, unfriendly and even hostile faces occupied the houses of my family and friends. I saw that it was not my town that I found but the graveless cemetery of my loved ones. Since then it has remained no more than the background of my first sixteen years.

My father, Feuerstein Miklós, was born in 1896, the second child of a family of two girls and four boys. He told me much about his childhood in the far-off peripheries of Kassa, about the friends, games, wanderings, and I think that it was a happy time for him until he was ten years old. After that, because there were no higher classes in their place, he had to move to the city, to his grandfather's, who was once a rich contractor until he nearly went bankrupt in no small measure because of my grandfather's (his son's) squandering as an army officer. It seems that this was the reason why there was not much goodwill between them, and relations between my father and his grandfather were strained. The period of time that my father had to stay at his grandfather's house was very difficult for him: he had to get up at four o'clock in the morning to milk the cows and deliver the milk before classes and never got a good word for his efforts. He refused to speak about these years, only that at the age of thirteen he left school and his grandfather's house and began to work as an apprentice in textile shops. He learned the trade and succeeded well enough, but was not really sorry that, in 1914 at the age of 18, the First World War broke out and he was conscripted. At the end of the war, in 1918, he was demobilised with the rank of first gunnery sergeant with orders of merit but, unlike his friends, he did not like to talk about his experiences in the Army or the war. His grandfather died during his service and, as far as I know, my father never visited his grave.

After demobilisation, my father returned to the place where he worked before the war, but this time as a shop assistant. Within a few years he had saved some money and, with the help of some loans, he opened his own store on Main Street in Kassa. He and my mother already knew each other and were sort of engaged, but they could not marry yet because they had not enough money. My father did not have many years of schooling, but he had a natural intelligence, was clever, daring, modern and open-minded. He was the first one in Kassa and in the whole of Slovakia to begin selling a newfangled and faintly scandalous invention: silk stockings for ladies. He was even the first to advertise in movie-houses and did it with an advertisement of his own design: on the screen you saw a head with a hole in it and the announcer said, (and you saw it on the screen too) 'You will have a hole in the head'. On the screen appeared a silk stocking with a hole in its head, and the text went on ' in your stocking if you don't buy it in Feuerstein's store'.

There was much talk and discussion about this as people wondered if it was in 'good taste' to show a head with a hole on the screen, and really, what was the connection between the two, but the slogan caught on and so did the new fashion. My father became the 'stocking king' and at last was able to marry my mother. Even thirty years later, here in Israel, there were aunties from my hometown who, instead of saying 'hello', would greeted me with 'you'll have a hole in your head'. Silk stockings, a wonderful invention. They had a seam on the back of the leg that became crooked and the ladies had to straighten it once in a while and, to straighten the seams properly, they had to hike the skirts up a bit. What a sight it was!

My mother, Etelka, born Altmann, was born in 1898 in Prešov, that is Eperjes in Hungarian, a small town some forty kilometres from Kassa. Her family was Orthodox, very religious, but educated and liberal, with a strong sentimental bond among the brothers and sisters. It was a bond, which was maintained, after my mother's marriage in Kassa, by frequent letters and visits. It was a family that loved and knew books, was somewhat formal and conventional, and even contacts within the family were bound by good manners and etiquette.

My parents got married in 1926 and I was born two years later. I was an only child, the youngest grandchild of both my father and my mother's family and, as such, without doubt, spoiled. After my birth, my mother stayed home. We always had a maid and for four years after my birth I had a German nurse too, because my mother wanted me to learn her second language and speak it without an accent.

My parents' social life was mostly within the family. Except for the weekly visit to the movies and seeing every Hungarian play that came 'down' from Budapest, they did not visit much. My father's family met nearly every Saturday afternoon in my grandparents' garden and on Sundays we went on a hike in the forest. When I was little, I used to walk with my father and in the winter we used a small sled. My father was a special man. As long as I can remember, he spoke with me earnestly as though I were a grown man. He asked me questions and discussed the answers. From a very early age he asked me questions in addition and subtraction and, by the time I entered first grade, I knew a good part of the multiplication table that he had taught me in our walks. He had a fur coat that was called at that time an urban fur-coat, which was fabric on the outside and fur on the inside, perhaps because of fashion or in order not to be ostentatious, I don't know. When in winter I walked with my father and got cold, I put my hand in the fur pocket of his coat to warm it and I shall never forget the feelings of secure tranquillity, pleasure and pride of those moments, which I have never felt since.

My father had another extraordinary trait that I learned to appreciate only much later: he answered all my questions with absolute honesty and without too many explanations. I could not have been more than three or four years old, I remember, when I asked him where babies came from, and he answered without hesitation or embarrassment that they came out of their mothers' bellies. His explanation was enough for me and I did not ask any more questions. When he did not know the answer, and that happened often enough, he would say that he did not know but that he would find out. The following day, when I had long since forgotten our conversation, he reminded me and said that the answer was such and such, or that he had not found the answer, but that we should think what the answer could be.

My mother, Etelka, was a delicate, beautiful, calm, blue-eyed, elegant woman and I don't remember her ever scolding me. It was not necessary because she had more effective educational ways. She was a walking lie detector. She only had to press my nose to know if I was telling the truth. She always said that, if I prevaricated, my nose got soft to the touch, and later when I read about criminal investigations I remember wondering why the detectives did not use my mother's much simpler method instead of the endless questioning. She even had a harder punishment. When I sat on her lap, I saw myself as in a mirror in her blue eyes. She said that if I had done something bad, I wouldn't be in her eyes. If I had a bad conscience about doing something I should not have done, I always ran to check if I was still in her eyes. I always was...

I don't know if she ever felt lonely in Kosice, the town of my father's family. When she married my father, she left a big loving family in Presov. She and my father were very different. When my mother became angry, which did not happen often, she got a headache. When my father became angry, the whole world knew about it and it made my mother uncomfortable because of the neighbours. My father, who did not mince his words, did not hesitate to let all who cared to know and some who did not, what his opinion of nosey neighbours was. My father forgot the whole thing after five minutes and could not for the life of him understand why my mother was still moody.

My father was proud of his outspokenness and made fun of my mother's family, the Altmanns adherence to the 'finicky' manners, sentimentality, idealism and straightness, that he called 'Altmania', a nickname, that interestingly caught on, and was frequently used even by them. Despite all that, Father was very proud of my mother and her family and even she secretly liked his unconventional outspokenness, even while scolding him for it.

Above all, there was a mutual respect, liking and a deep love between the two of them. There is no greater, more beautiful, and everlasting gift for a child, that gives him more security, than the knowledge, that his parents love not only him, but each other too.

Ilus Licht, a daughter of Mother's sister, Gina and her husband Philip from Eperjes, was an integral part of our family. She went to school and later worked in Kassa and stayed with us. She was thirteen years older than me and was like a beloved older sister, a feeling that was shared by my parents. She got her fair share of my father's remarks concerning the Altmanns and the differences between the two families. Ilus did not hold back her retorts and enjoyed the full support of my mother. She was very shortsighted and it was, according to my father, the cause of many embarrassing accidents that he never got tired of retelling.

Theoretically, she had her own room, but in practice she sat with us, or I sat in her room. Despite the great difference in age, there was a mutual love between us. I even loved her family, who lived in Eperjes, very much and when visiting the Altmanns, I mostly stayed with them. Even Ilus' brothers and sisters did everything to make my visit pleasant and dragged me along everywhere.

I must have been about five years old when Ilus had an admirer, by the name of György Feri. He was a journalist, but also the publisher, owner, reporter, chief redactor and the errand boy of a weekly called *The Truth*, a name that was in direct contrast with its contents. Feri, in his own words, earned his bread by what he wrote, but the butter on his bread he earned by what he was 'convinced' not to write. Toward Ilus he had certain aspirations that my parents did not like very much, and they didn't hesitate to share with her their feelings that, in spite of her liberal and progressive views, it was customary to save virginity for the wedding night. Therefore, I got instructions, without explanations, to stay with the two of them, and not to leave them for a moment. But Feri was not a journalist for nothing and had refined solution: as he knew about Ilus' weakness for me, he tried to use it. In the next number of *The Truth* there appeared an interview on a whole page, with picture and everything, with the title: 'Interview with a Five Year Old Infant Prodigy' full of my smart sayings. The number of copies was double that week because my mother sent it to everyone within the families, with all their fringes, and everyone she ever spoke to. The relations with Feri improved significantly. If this strategy worked with Ilus as well, I wouldn't know.

Some years later, Ilus and I read together the famous Hungarian poets Ady, Arany, and other classics. World literature and chiefly poetry lose very much from the fact that the Hungarian language is so different from all the European language families, and its cadence is very strange to all who do not speak it. I have Ilus to thank for that, to this very day, I remember kilometres of Hungarian poetry and folksongs by heart and sing them with great gusto.

I was about twelve years old, the age when the blood begins to boil and, because my room was near the bathroom, I peeked in when Ilus was washing herself. She caught me in the act. She stormed out, naked – the good news – and fetched me two mighty blows in the face – the bad news. The pain was bad and the shame was worse, but Ilus did not tell my parents. Later, when she saw that I did not dare to come near her, she called me and explained that at my age it is only natural to peek on girls. Of course, I asked, as I had the right to, if so then why the blows and she explained that nothing is more right and natural than to beat somebody caught peeking. I accepted it without rancour and never peeked at Ilus again; only at the maid.

I was some three or four years old when my grandfather decided to sell his tavern and with my father's help he bought a house with five apartments and a big garden in Kassa. They lived from the rent. They had a two-room apartment on the first floor with another, separate room, where my father's two younger unmarried brothers, Mano and Rudi, lived. The third brother, Árpád, was already married and lived in another town in Slovakia. He, his wife and three small daughters were murdered in Auschwitz. Mano was the superintendent of a big shoe store but in 1939 was called up and never came back. Rudi, my favourite and youngest uncle, went to Prague and was murdered there by the Germans.

My father's younger sister, Manyi, her husband, Henrik Schapira and their little girl, Yuditka, lived in the second apartment on the first floor. Henrik was the local manager of Tatra's automobile store and as such sometimes brought home a car for the weekends so both our families went for a spin, to my great happiness. Henrik, like his other Jewish contemporaries, was called up to Labour Service in the Hungarian Army and was crushed by a tank. Manyi and Yuditka, who were six or seven then, went with us to Auschwitz and were murdered there. In the mezzanine there were three other Jewish families who shared our destiny. The basement flat was for the janitor and his wife who did the necessary reparations and helped grandfather in the garden and grandmother in the kitchen. Father's elder sister, Aliz, her husband Berti Goldberg and their two teenage daughters, Marta and Kato, lived not far away. They went with us to Auschwitz. Only the two girls survived.

The garden was Grandfather's pride, joy and daily occupation. In its middle, from the garden door to the bower, there was a pebble-strewn path. On one side there was a row of gooseberry bushes and behind that a row of red and white roses. A long, whitewashed stake supported every bush with a coloured glass ball on its head.

On the other side of the path there was a row of redcurrant bushes, and behind them two apple trees, two pea (pea is the correct word, as they were pea trees) trees, one peach and a sour cherry tree. After the trees and on the sides of the bower there were multicoloured and fragrant flowerbeds. My father had built the bower, a wooden pavilion, and had planted grapes and blue flowered creepers on its side. Inside there were self-made wooden benches around a long, rough-hewn table. On Saturday afternoons, weather permitting, the whole family sat there, and nearly always Boehm Elek and her daughter Zsuzsika, who was my age, were there too. Elek was the brother-in-law of Father's older sister, Aliz, a very good friend and companion on the Sunday picnics. Near the bower there was a big swing, also Father's work, for us children, but the parents used it too, among much merriment.

What did we do, sitting there? I really don't know. We ate and drank homemade goodies and lemonade, fruit that fell off the trees. The men talked about politics, the women about the children, domestic matters and the newest scandals. Zsuzsika and I told each other the news in our high schools – there were separate ones for boys and girls. I don't remember ever being bored and everyone loved these Saturday afternoons.

After Father's younger brothers were drafted to Labour Service, their room gradually became a storeroom for the fruit. Omama and Opapa, as we called our grandparents, stored the fruit in such a way that the ones with a small blemish should be the first ones to be used. Once, in the course of a summer rainstorm, the lightning struck one of the big, old pear trees, and it seemed that it was burnt. Spring came and with it a miracle: a third of the big tree burst into flower. The tree had always been full of small, average pears, but after the lightning it bore no more than thirty or forty fruit but each and every one of them was huge, yellow, full of juice and tasted like paradise. Omama decided right then and there that these pears were only for me and woe befell anyone

THE TUMBLER

else who dared touch them. When I sank my teeth into one of
them, the sweet juice squirted in my eyes, and even today I can
feel their taste and the pangs of conscience that only I was
allowed to taste them.

On Sundays we usually we went on picnics and outings with
the same company as on the Saturday afternoons. Sometimes
Elsa, the daughter of my mother's elder brother, Uncle Sandor,
her husband Eugen Biedermann and their son, Gustika, who was
two years younger than me, came with us too. Dushika, Elsa's
young, unmarried sister, could very seldom be persuaded to join
us but, when she came, there was no trouble at all in persuading
Rudi, my father's young brother, to come along too. From all
these relatives, only Elsa survived the Holocaust. Uncle Zoltan
Altmann, my mother's elder brother, his wife Erna and their
children Erzsike and Izso joined us only when there was not much
walking because Erna had trouble with her heart. Erzsike married
Imre Gerstel and emigrated to Palestine before the war. Izso was
murdered in Labour Service and Zoltan was murdered in
Auschwitz.

These outings were, as a rule, walking tours in the forest, from
the Csermely towards and over Banko. Sometimes we sat down to
rest near one of the many creeks, and built small dams from
stones that in no time created a small bathing pond for us
children. Sometimes only my mother, father and I went cycling to
Gajda where there was a mineral water spring, a not very clean
swimming pool and shadowy benches and tables to rest. The real
feasts and happiest occasions for me were the weekends when
Henri was allowed to bring home a car and the two families drove
to the railway tunnel near the Hernad River, where there was a
sandy beach and slow-flowing water to bathe in. For me, the best
and proudest moments were the drives there and back as I got to
sit by the driver's side and was responsible for the old fashioned
hooter that was a horn under the side mirror. The summit of
satisfaction was to meet some of my envious pedestrian friends
and pass by, hooting in a cloud of dust with the car racing at the
incredible speed of at least thirty kilometres per hour.

Azriel Feuerstein

In the summer holidays we hired a room in the neighbouring Slovak village, Kostolany nad Hernadom. The house was near the railway station and the dam on the Hernad. There, my mother and I were alone for four days a week. We swam behind the dam or sat on it in the shallow water and did not tire of seeing the fish swim by. From an old underskirt I had made a net and sometimes succeeded in catching a fish that was not careful enough, but I did not have the heart to kill it, and neither did my mother, so we let it swim away.

Father arrived on the Friday afternoon train, and for him it was no problem to kill the fish and clean them. We caught a couple of nice ones, and without cleaning their scales we packed each one in clay wrapping. After that we went down to the fields to steal some corncobs. We prepared the fire carefully and, before igniting it, we put in the clay-clad fish and sat down in the shade to wait and then put the pieces of sausages that we had rolled in newspapers into the fire. We cleaned the corn, because my mother was afraid of bugs, then put them back in their leaves and placed them on the glowing embers. The corn went in last and came out first, black and sooty. My father said that we should wait until the sausages were ready too, but who had the patience? We ate it sooty as it was, sweet and half done. By then the smell of the sausages became very appetizing, and with the corn leaves that were left for that purpose, we cleaned the sausages and ate them with a big slice of fresh bread, but slowly because the best was before us yet. We were not very hungry any more, so we waited until the fire burned down and took out the burned pieces of clay from the embers and with a small stone broke them into two. The scales of the fish were glued to the now brick-like clay, and there was the white fish, cooked and needing only a pinch of salt. After that feast, fit for a king, we went down to the water to wash ourselves and Mother always found something more on both my father and me that needed cleaning.

I often had tonsillitis and it was decided that my tonsils had to be removed. I had to go to the Jewish hospital in Budapest, Hungary, which was a foreign country then. In Budapest we stayed with my mother's older sister, Frida and her husband Edy Altmann. They had an apartment together with their daughter, Boske and her husband Bandi Varga, who was a travelling salesman and was seldom at home. It was a then very big, five room apartment, and there was enough space because Boske's two younger brothers had a room together not far away. These two young men were called up for Labour Service in 1942, the youngest one, Laci, in 1944. Neither of them came back.

My tonsils were removed under anaesthesia, and I had to stay in the hospital another day. I was forbidden to speak, but had to eat ice cream. I followed this order to the best of my ability and with much enthusiasm. It is true that we had ice cream in Kassa too, and we even had a genuine Italian gelateria, but in Budapest there was something new: ice cream on sticks. I did my best to reduce the stock and tried every kind. There was something else in Budapest that was as yet unknown in Kassa: ice-cold milk, sold in small bottles in the parks, and I tried that too with pleasure. After some days of convalescence, we boarded the train in the evening and arrived in the morning at Siofok, near the lake of Balaton. On the train I woke up early in the morning, as the first rays of the sun fell on endless fields of watermelons, every one of which weighing thirty kilos or more. These enormous watermelons stood before the store doors in Budapest and were sold in pieces. I have never seen anything like them again. We had some nice days near Balaton Lake, swimming, sightseeing and basking in the sun, and we even went to try out the echo in Tihany. When we came back to Kassa, I was only sorry that I had no more tonsils to be removed. I was in Budapest two more times: once with my mother, and once, at the age of thirteen, alone!

Meeting friends whom I knew from kindergarten filled the weekday afternoons and the long winter evenings. Gelman Zoli, my best friend, a handsome, tall and a bit reticent but very funny boy, who spent the summer vacations working on his grandparents' holdings in the village and who was full of exciting tales about the peasant girls there; Fischer Gyuri, who was called Pista. When very young he got infant paralysis, survived, but walked and spoke with difficulty. He was a poet and a translator. At the age of fifteen he translated Edgar Allan Poe's 'The Raven', which had been done countless times before him, but his translation was outstanding. Despite his invalidity, he somehow survived Auschwitz but starved to death in KZ Dornau. The fearless Edelyi Feri led our battles with anti-Semites and was our secretary in the Zionist organisation. There were twenty-two Jews in our class. Eighteen did not survive. A whole world, gone forever.

5

Pictures from Home

'Välkommen, Fröken Ulle, I really had no hope to see you in such nasty weather,' I cheerfully said.

'So you thought me a fair-weather friend? That is not nice,' replied Fröken Ulle in mock overtones of being hurt by my words.

'But, as you see, I hoped that you wouldn't forget and got the pictures ready.'

This time the conversation about the weather was shorter than usual and even the mandatory coffee ceremony was somewhat hurried.

'Did you have time, Fröken Ulle, to begin reading my book?'

'Yes, Yeory. I have nearly finished the first part, but had some trouble with the many foreign names.'

I knew that these names wouldn't be easy for the non-Hungarian readers, but I felt it was my duty towards those whose destiny touched mine to record their names.

It is true that this book is chiefly my story and, in some measure, that of my contemporaries, but let at least some of the names remind us of them, the millions, who were destroyed, without compassion, without names, without burial.

Not only were they not remembered, but also a world power at that time did its very best that even their ashes should not be found. In the end they were beaten, and they still hastily, in the wake of defeat, tried to cover their tracks, albeit unsuccessfully.

I hope that my readers, and Fröken Ulle, won't hold it against me that I have changed some of the names.

'Yeory, let's see the pictures.'

THE TUMBLER

As I showed the photos to Fröken Ulle I said, 'The pictures[*] of my maternal grandparents[1] you have seen before, and here is my grandfather's[2] obituary which was on the first page of my mother's and her sisters' album.'

'I can understand the pride of the family very well and it is not nice of you to make fun of it,' Fröken Ulle sternly said.

'True, I was always a cynic,' I replied.

'Who is that nice blond child here?'

'If my mother put it in her album, it must be me, before I got fat and my hair turned dark. On my right is my father, and on my left my German nurse, Irma[3].'

'Thank you very much for the explanation, but somehow I think that I could have found out by myself who is who. And your hair is not dark but light brown, and you are not fat at all.'

I was dumbfounded. She was right: now I am not fat at all. Grete (she is not part of this story) always told me that she liked me for my blue eyes, and the 'salt-cellars' on both sides of my neck. It is interesting that I still thought of myself as fat.

'And this Irma,' asked Fröken Ulle, 'where was she born and how long did she stay with you?'

'She was born in a small village near Hamburg and stayed with us for four years because my mother wanted my pronunciation to be truly German. When she left, we both wept but I still sound Hungarian in every language.'

I knew right from the beginning where the wind was blowing from regarding this conversation, because Fröken Ulle let me understand many times that she did not like my behaviour towards Anna-Lisa. She was a nice looking German girl, who worked in the kitchen, and many times tried to get me into conversation, and, perhaps more. I for my part let her politely understand that I didn't need any German friends. I was not alone in this: there was a Norwegian boy, Kurt, who felt the same as I.

---

[*] The images given reference numbers in this text can be seen in the plate section within this book. They are each numbered to match the reference numbers throughout the text.

Azriel Feuerstein

'You and Kurt, you are unable to understand, that there are good Germans too,' Fröken Ulle said persuasively.

'Indeed, there are. What is more, they are the only nation whose human qualities can be measured objectively,' I coldly replied.

'Now, that is nonsense, Yeory. How could moral qualities be objectively measured? That is impossible.'

'Very simply, Fröken Ulle. You only have to dig him up, and measure how deep he lies. The deeper the grave, the better the German.'

Her usually white cheeks reddened suddenly, and there were sparks of anger that flashed in her blue eyes.

'You and Kurt! Are you two really unable to understand, that you cannot condemn a whole nation or group in its entirety? You hate a whole nation, like you do the Nazis. A nation that, through ages, contributed to and enriched European literature, poetry, music, science and everything.'

'That is true, Fröken Ulle,' I replied as I kissed her hand with real regret. 'Believe me, in my mind I understand it too. And anyway, we should not hurt your feelings. But please, understand ours. It is too soon for Kurt, whose brother the Germans hanged, to accept this and it is certainly too soon for me.'

Fröken Ulle blushed lightly, turned away, and began to potter with the coffee cups as she reinforced what she had just said, 'Make sure that you understand it, and the sooner the better. The Almighty did not give us brains, sense and intelligence so that we would be ruled by hate and thirst for vengeance. But let us leave all that for now, and return to the pictures.'

'That one is of my parents[4] and I before our trip to Budapest, when I was six.'

'What elegance! You see, in this picture you are really plump. A really nice family!'

'We were, Fröken Ulle, we were. Here, I am two years old walking in Kassa with my father in his urban fur coat[5] that I have so many memories of. Here, I am four or five years old with my father on the swing[6] in my grandparents' garden. On the back of this picture are the date and my name in Mother's dear handwriting. This one is a picture of our store[7]. Standing in the doorway are Father, Mr Huebsch, the bookkeeper, and Margit the shop assistant. Marcsa is sitting in the forefront, at the edge of the sidewalk, selling flowers. In winter she sold roasted chestnuts, sitting on a chair, with a pot full of embers under her voluminous skirts.

'Here is my grandfather[8], for once without his pipe that was normally never out of his mouth. This pipe was full of "virgin tobacco" that was illegal tax-free tobacco. Virgin it may have been, but it stank to high heaven and drove away both people and animals. My father always quarrelled with him, saying that for a few pennies that he saved on taxes he could land in jail.'

Fröken Ulle let slip when she said, 'It seems that these old men are the same everywhere. Just imagine, Yeory, my grandfather does not smoke but has an illegal distillery at home. What a shame it would be for the family if he gets caught! Don't even think about telling it to anyone.'

'Fröken Ulle, we shall both bury our families' dark secrets in our hearts forever.'

'Enough of idle chatter, let's return to the pictures,' directed Fröken Ulle.

'At your service, Fröken Ulle. Here[9] is Grandma, Father's younger sister Manyi and her husband, Henrik Schapira, Gusti, Elza's son, and my mother and I. What is not shown in this picture is that, as in all the others, I am the only survivor.

'In that one[10], Mother and I are at Lake Balaton, and on the back of the picture, my mother wrote that it was after my tonsillectomy. Here[11] is Mother in the garden with the roses.'

With a trace of pain in her voice Fröken Ulle said, 'Not so fast, Yeory. I like to take my time looking at the pictures. It is nice to see a family sticking together.

'Here in Sweden, after the children are married, they do not often return home and maintain such a close relationship with their parents and with each other. That mostly happens only on special occasions.'

Azriel Feuerstein

'Yes, that is true, but don't forget that at that time there were not many alternative pastimes for family picnics,' I replied.

I returned to talking my way through the pictures, 'That is Father with Zsuzsika, Elek Boehm's daughter, and I[12] in a brook. Mother always said that she didn't want this picture in her album because Father looks "ordinary" but it seems that she did not have the heart to throw it away.

'Here is Rudi, Dusika, Manyi and Father.[13] Rudi was Father's youngest brother and my favourite uncle; he took me on walks and taught me many songs in Hungarian and Czech. He seldom came to our outings, but always when Dusika came too.

'This picture[14] was taken when I was two years old and I am not in it. Here is Izso, the son of Erna and Zoltan Altmann, Mother's older brother and Laci, a cousin, Alize Goldberg, Father's older sister and her two daughters, Marta and Kato, Manyi, Father's younger sister, and my parents.

'Izso had a birthmark on his forehead that gave him a very romantic look and made him the darling of the girls. He was enlisted and murdered in the Hungarian Labour Service and all the others died in Auschwitz. Only Erna died in her own bed.'

'You see, Yeory, in situations such as yours, the only thing that helps is faith and being aware that we, with our limited human knowledge, cannot and should not even try to understand the will of God and His hidden purposes for his actions.

'We have to trust Him and can only mourn those who are not with us anymore, who died as martyrs with God's name on their lips.'

'Fröken Ulle, if somebody survived Auschwitz and still believes in God, he must be an atheist.'

Her face mirrored a deep sorrow and real fear as she said, 'But He saved you from there! And what do you mean saying, that by believing in Him, you have to be a denier of Him?'

'Fröken Ulle, from Auschwitz nobody was saved, we were a few, who survived it. And what I mean is, that if you believe that what happened there and other places like it, happened with God's knowledge, permission or out of His neglectfulness, you

45

THE TUMBLER

attribute to Him qualities, whose attribution to God is tantamount of denying Him.

'And about them, who died there. You called them "martyrs". Martyrs, Fröken Ulle? Saints?! True, that is what we call them, but they were not saints. They were ordinary everyday people, good and bad. Martyrs?! They did not walk willingly to their death, and would have done everything to remain alive, as any normal person would, if they only had had a way out. We call them martyrs and saints, to lighten our pain and give a meaning, as it were, to their meaningless and unexplainable deaths.

'What makes me most afraid, even more than the carnage that was planned and executed in a most painful and humiliating manner, is that the planners and executors of this unthinkably horrible crime, were ordinary people. People like you and me, sitting in their ordinary offices, working from nine to five like everybody else, drinking their coffee, like we do now, and planning how to carry out the unthinkable in the most efficient way.

'I would like to see them as monsters, but I am afraid that they were not monsters and I did not see them as such; I did not see them as mass murderers with blood on their hands. Some of them liked music, I am sure, and nature, and were able to embrace their children after a day's work at the office. While stroking their daughters' blonde hair, they reflected whether the victims' hair should be shorn off before or after the gas chamber. People who are able to tell themselves that it was God's will and leave it at that are lucky.

'This choice was not given to me. Our prayer for the dead, the Kadish, mentions neither the dead nor the bereavement; it is full of the glorification of God and extolling His mercy. It is the first duty of an orphan to recite this prayer for the salvation of the souls of the dead. I was unable to recite this prayer and thus accept the fate of my parents and my people.'

Fröken Ulle wiped her eyes that were red from tears and said, 'Your first duty is to recite this prayer at once. You have to ask yourself what your parents would expect from you, and do it. I,

46

thank God, was not in such a situation, or even one like it, but I too know bereavement and mourning and irreplaceable loss, and I have always felt that prayer helps more than anything else, and I'll pray for you too.'

'Thank you for your good heart, Fröken Ulle, and forgive me for making you sad with things that should not concern you.'

'As the poet said, "man is not an island" and if such things happen, they should concern everyone. See you, Yeory, and all the best.'

She left, and I regretted the whole conversation. She, poor soul, had nothing to do with all that had happened to us and I was wrong to make her sad. Anyway, she is unable to understand, as is any normal person who was not there. Her country did more for the Jews than nearly any other nation. Even then, when it was dangerous, when the empire of evil was at the summit of its might, Sweden with the help of the Norwegian and Danish underground rescued many of the Jews from those German occupied lands and took them into their country, in the middle of the war when the doors of all other countries were firmly shut and accepting them was no small danger. It is true that they traded with the Germans, but with the other side too. After the war they helped thousands to return to life. No wonder some of them asked themselves whether the Germans had a rational reason for hating the Jews. They did not understand that the Holocaust was a fateful meeting between the ideal murderer, the German Nazi, and the ideal victim, the always-persecuted Jew.

6

Historical Background and Warnings

This part of the story is for those people who, incredible as it may seem, are not well versed in the history and geography of Central Europe between the two World Wars.

This period and place are not easy to understand, even for those who lived there at that time. Therefore, it is important to talk about it while telling the story of a family whose destiny was closely bound with, and we can say determined by, that time and that place.

The First World War ended in 1918 with the defeat of Germany and the Austro-Hungarian Empire with the division of the latter into many national states by the victors, who wanted them to be as homogenous as possible in language and nationality. That is how the states of Rumania, Yugoslavia and Czechoslovakia were born. Despite the good intentions of the victors, these states were very far from being homogenous.

On the very border of Czechoslovakia with Germany, there was a wide zone, the Sudeten, with German inhabitants. In the Slovak part of that country there lived Slovaks, Hungarians, Germans and Ukrainians near each other with their mutual dislike slowly simmering on a low fire that erupted on Saturday nights in occasional knifings in the taverns. If all these peoples had one thing in common, it was the low regard they all felt towards their Jewish neighbours living amongst them.

This anti-Semitism surfaced mostly in anti-Jewish jokes that the Jews laughed at no less than the others, and occasional Jew-baiting that was frowned on in better circles. The saying was that an anti-Semite is one who hates the Jews *more* than necessary, and the Jews accepted this too. They thought that things should not be blown out of proportion.

In Hungary, after its division, there was a communist revolution that was led by a Jew, Bela Kun, who was defeated by the 'whites' of Admiral Miklos Horthy, supported by the foreign Rumanian Army. Horthy proclaimed himself Regent and Head of State and Hungary remained thus nominally a Monarchy, led by a Regent. In the course of the fighting with the communists, some parts of Horthy's army staged pogroms with 'only' fifty dead, but these pogroms (Russian term, originally meaning 'riot', that came to be applied to a series of violent attacks on Jews in Russia) were conducted in such a cruel, bestial way that they remained unrivalled until the Nazis. Hungary was the first state in Europe to introduce anti-Jewish laws, long before the Nazis were even known. These laws, limiting the number of Jews in universities (Numerus Clausus), were accepted by the Hungarian Parliament in 1920. The pogroms during the anti-communist struggle one did not talk about. The 'right' people could circumvent the new laws and the Hungarian Jews did not let themselves be bothered about them. They remained quiet, patriotic and loyal, and tried to forget everything.

As a significant percentage of the middle-class in Kassa, the Jews remained Hungarians in their hearts and feelings in spite of the fact that Kassa now belonged to the Czechoslovakian state, under the name of Košice. The worldwide depression made itself felt in our town too but there was a tranquil optimism in the atmosphere, and a feeling of security that the people and nations had learned their lesson from the destruction of the last war and that there could not be another war between the leading nations, come what may.

However, all that was slowly changing with the emerging Nazi propaganda, while things began to snowball after Hitler came to power in 1933. The Western Powers, who saw Hitler only as a counterweight to Bolshevism and the Soviets, closed their eyes to the massive German rearming that was forbidden by the peace agreements after the First World War. They endured without protest the bloodthirsty propaganda against the post-war borders that were the results of Germany losing the war and they hoped that the renascent German power would threaten the Soviet Union and not them.

In March 1936 Hitler spat for the first, but not the last, time into the eyes of the great Western Powers and chiefly in the eyes of France. Some weeks after a speech promising peace, the German Army broke into the neutral and strategically important Rheinland that at that time was under French administration. The German troops had an explicit order to retreat at once at the first sign of resistance. The French did not even protest and Hitler learned the lesson. In 1938 he annexed Austria into the Third Reich without even firing a shot. A short time after that he put on the international agenda the question of Czechoslovakia by inciting the Sudeten-Germans living in Czechoslovakia in a zone by the German border. This German minority through the leader of their Nazi party, Heinlein, was wholly under Hitler's influence and demanded the right to 'return to the Reich' because of alleged anti-German discriminations by the Czechs. The Czechoslovakian fortifications were in that area, ready, manned and no less mighty than the French Maginot Line.

Czechoslovakia mobilised its Army and held civil defence exercises against bombings. Within the framework of these exercises in our town, my father brought home from the shop a small cardboard pipe, painted red to represent the bomb, a bucket of water and a hand-pump with a two-metre long hose. My mother energetically handled the pump; I held the hose and the bomb soon disintegrated. My modesty would forbid me to tell about my heroic role in the defence of Czechoslovakia – I was ten years old at that time – if it were not for the fact that this episode, six years later, nearly caused my untimely death in Hildesheim. It is my woeful duty, however, to relate, that my tireless efforts for Czechoslovakia did not meet with any greater success than the work of the statesmen of the Western Powers. Hitler had decided months before that the dismembering of Czechoslovakia should begin, one way or the other, in September. His generals were so convinced that the Western Powers would interfere and bring about the sure defeat of Germany that they decided in that case to remove and arrest Hitler and retreat at once. That was not the case and so the last opportunity to avoid the Second World War and its monstrosities was missed.

There was no Western interference. Neville Chamberlain, Britain's Prime Minister at the time, ran down the steps of his aeroplane, waving a paper and shouting 'Peace in our time', and was cheered by the public. This occurred on 30 September 1938, after the shameful conference in Munich that decided the fate of Czechoslovakia. In the first days of October the Germans occupied the Sudeten zone in Czechoslovakia with all its fortifications, with the blessings of Great Britain and France. In November, Hungary and Poland received their respective parts of the dismembered Czechoslovakia as their award for siding with Hitler. At the same time, the Czech part of the land came under Hitler's 'protection' as the Czech Protectorate, including its car, aeroplane and arms industries, and Slovakia became an 'independent' Nazi-clerical state. Hitler accomplished all this, without firing one shot, or losing one soldier. One year later, in 1939, without opposition and with the enthusiastic support of his generals who saw in him a genius, he attacked Poland, wrongly assuming that the Western Powers would not interfere even this time, and thus the Second World War began.

Even before that, in November 1938, a Jewish student in Paris, Herschel Grünspann, whose parents were murdered by the Germans, killed a German diplomat in their embassy in Paris. That gave the Germans a pretext for a period of pogroms and destruction of Jewish properties under the name of 'Kristallnacht'. In those days some thirty Jews were killed, many wounded and beaten, and hundreds of synagogues, Jewish shops and properties burned; many thousands of Jews, chiefly rich ones, were sent to the concentration camps in order to facilitate the robbing of their property and make them understand that they should emigrate which, in itself, became more difficult by the day. This warning was directed towards all the Jews in Europe and in Hungary, and Kassa too, but we all had more important things to think about.

As I wrote before, in November 1938 Kassa, with parts of former Slovakia, was given to Hungary after the so-called Vienna Decision. Kassa had at that time some seventy thousand inhabitants, of whom twelve thousand were Jews. The best of Kassa's middle class and a great part of the Jews awaited the change of the regime with true enthusiasm and greeted Miklos Horthy's entry on his white horse at the head of the parade with patriotic fervour. My family too was among the cheering multitude and last, but not least, was I, who in addition to national aspirations had my worries about the bad grades in Slovak language in my high-school class.

A Latin proverb that, I am afraid I shall have to cite on more occasions, says that the gods, when wanting to destroy somebody, first make him blind. For no one is this proverb truer than for the Hungarian Jews in these years, and for our family who, the more threatening the signs got, so our eyes closed ever so more tightly.

To tell the truth, in Kassa it was as if everything remained the same. In our high-school class of forty, we were twenty-one Jews. We got registered in 1938, when Kassa was still in Czechoslovakia, and it remained unchanged in the coming years. But in the class below us, which registered under Hungarian laws, only three Jews were accepted according to the Hungarian Numerus Clausus law. At that time, the Hungarians began to review Jews' citizenship papers.

There were many Jewish families that had come from Poland many years, and sometimes generations previously, but until then did not have the time or the money to think about their citizenship, and were faced with a big problem. Among them, there was an orthodox Chassidic family, named Abrahamovits, who had a son my age, named Bumi, and we used to play together. They lived on the ground floor in our house, in a small two-room apartment.

In September 1939, Hitler attacked Poland. Great Britain and France came to its defence and thus the Second World War started. Poland was defeated in two months. Even before that, we had heard no end of bad news from Germany. We heard that the passports and identity cards of the Jews were stamped with a red 'J', that the Jews had to wear a yellow star, that they were building concentration camps, that the Jews were being dismissed from work and that their stores were being taken away from them. This news was very disturbing, of course, but it was, after all, so far away. In 1940, all the Jews who had no Hungarian citizenship, even if they were long-time inhabitants of Kassa, were conscripted and deported to Kamenec-Podolsk in Poland. Our old neighbours, the Abrahamovits family, were among them. Were we bothered very much about all this? Did we talk about it at mealtimes? I don't remember that we did. Some months later, there were rumours that they were all shot. What kind of absurd, alarming tales! Shot?! Why would the Germans shoot them?

The new border between Hungary and Slovakia ran now between Kassa, the town of my father's family that was now Hungary, and Eperjes, that is Prešov, with Mother's family now in Slovakia. From my father's brothers, only Arpad, who was married there, his wife and three daughters lived in Slovakia. That land was then under much tighter German supervision than Hungary and had stricter anti-Jewish laws under the prime minister and Catholic priest Tiso and his bloody-handed interior minister Sanyo Mach. The postal service between the two countries got more problematic. The letters were opened and censored on both sides of the border. The Jews were afraid of every superfluous word. The letters did not stop arriving but got shorter, with an occasional illegal, uncensored one that brought only bad news that got worse every time, and we knew that the Jews' situation there was growing worse every day.

In Kassa, there was no discernible change. The Jewish youths who came of age, and were conscripted for military service, did not get arms and served in the Labour Service, with a yellow armband on their uniform. They got debasing and degrading treatment, but every new recruit got more or less the same. Later, the military uniforms were taken away from the Jews and they had to bring clothes from home. The Jewish communities took care of these needs. Later, a conscription of the somewhat older men with families began, but there was a war on and the non-Jews were called up too.

The news from Eperjes was threatening and difficult to understand. We heard that they had closed the stores of the Jews and that their radios were taken away. In 1941 they began to concentrate the Jews in ghettos. We heard that Klari, Ilus' sister, got married, to Artur Sedlak, without being engaged before and that they lived in his village, Giraltovce. Without engagement?! It's very odd, isn't it? It is true there were rumours of unmarried young girls being sent away for work, but still, getting married right away...

Then we heard that it was true: the young girls, including Ancsi and Lilly, the younger sisters of Ilus and Klari, were taken to the railway station and their hair shorn off. They were clothed in thin, blue and white striped pyjamas and taken away to...Auschwitz?! What is this? Well, of course, it is not easy. But how long can the war last? Now that America joined the Allied Forces, certainly not long. Until their hair grows back, they'll be home, for sure.

In the meantime, in Kassa, life went on. True, Father got conscripted to Labour Service, and Mother cried the whole day, but luckily Father knew the doctor there and for a 'nominal and symbolic' sum he was declared unfit for service and sent home the same day. In the store, there was no change. There were ration cards now, but bread we baked privately at home and there were muffins for breakfast as before. There were no great changes in school either. We were in the fifth form and, as seniors, had the right to wear a golden stripe on our cap instead of the four silver ones. The teachers, who were now professors, continued to call us fools and assorted names but had to do it now with the prefix 'Mr' before our name and speak in the third person, as a matter of respect, like this: 'Mr Feuerstein is a fool, is that the way he submits homework?' You see? More respect.

Some soldiers returning from the Russian front for a furlough told some incredible tales. They said that the whole Jewish population of a village, men, women and children, old and young were led to the middle of a forest, to mass graves, that had been prepared for that purpose beforehand, forced to strip naked, and all shot into the grave, one on another. Is something like that possible? Of course not, a sick fantasy. Anyway, the war was nearly over.

In a tightly closed room, we listened to the BBC. It did not have much encouraging news. Hitler had enforced a 'peace treaty' with the French collaborators and inspected a parade of his forces in Paris. Yugoslavia, The Netherlands and Belgium were occupied; Norway and Denmark were under the German yoke.

England stood alone and prepared for invasion, enduring daily bombings on an unimaginable scale. At last! Hitler attacked the Soviet Union. There he would get his neck broken, like Napoleon before him.

7 December 1941. The Japanese attack Pearl Harbour and at last America was at war. But there is still no good news. The Japanese occupy the British and American colonies, one after the other. Singapore falls. They say that the Germans have difficulties on the Russian Front. It seems that the Russian winter is doing its work.

The BBC doesn't tell much about the Jews. Once or twice we hear about the killing of Jews and Russian prisoners of war. We know that the BBC is mostly trustworthy, but it is clear that in these cases it is propaganda, plain and simple.

Hitler comes, Hitler goes, but you have to remember that the Germans are a European 'Kulturvolk' and no murderers of babies. And now, at last, the beginning of the end: the fight in Stalingrad ended with the unconditional surrender of the Germans and two hundred thousand of them marched towards Siberia, as prisoners of war, with Marshal Paulus at their head.

But, strangely, in spite of all this, the war continues. We hear that the Jewish youth of the Zionist organisations in Slovakia seek ways to escape to Budapest and that even some Jews from Poland succeeded. They got help secretly from the Jewish community but were strictly warned not to spread 'rumours' and panic.

Azriel Feuerstein

In April 1943 we heard for the first time the words, 'the Warsaw Ghetto'. It seemed there were fights there. The Germans were bombing the ghetto. They destroyed the ghetto.

June or July, a calm, tranquil, restful Saturday. All three of us, Mother, Father and I, sit and eat the Shabbat midday meal (we were only three because Ilus was working). Everything was as usual: the white tablecloth, the sabbatical porcelain set, the Friday night candlesticks on the table. My father prepares his special sauce for the salad that he learned at the Italian Front in the First World War and is the only 'kitchen work' he ever performs. The domestic, Marish, is serving the meat soup. Everything was as usual.

Suddenly, without knocking(!), in rushes Boehm Elek, white as a sheet. Now, Elek is our very best friend. He and his daughter Zsuzsika are regular and welcome guests in our grandparents' garden on Shabbat afternoons as well as at our Sunday picnics, but all that did not mean that you might rush in, unceremoniously, in the middle of a Saturday meal. Without knocking(!).

First of all to calm him down, he got a glass of water from Mother, who sent Marish out with a gesture and made Elek sit down. He was breathing more or less normally and said that he was coming from the Joint (that is what the orphanage was called), and that there he met a boy in his late teens, who had escaped after the destruction of the Warsaw Ghetto through sewage channels and, after many dangers, managed to reach Hungary. He tells Elek that the systematic and well-planned extermination of the Jews began right after the German invasion of Poland, first in villages and smaller places, by special units of the SS that were established for that purpose. They took the whole Jewish population of the place, babies, women, and old men, sick and healthy, every single one, and shot them all into deep trenches after they were ordered to strip naked. Later special extermination camps were built, where the Jews were transported to from the ghettoes and killed in gas chambers. He told Elek that, at the time of the uprising in the Warsaw Ghetto, less than a third of the population remained as the rest had been transported and gassed in Treblinka. Now the captured ones, after the destruction of the Ghetto, were being transported to a newly built huge extermination camp, Auschwitz, where people are killed in gas chambers and their corpses burned in crematoriums. Auschwitz? Where did I hear that name before? And the most important thing, according to the boy, was to sell everything and flee, without thinking much about it, because Hungary was now the last country in Europe where there are Jews, but that it wouldn't remain so for long. Simply, sell everything, without telling it to anyone, buy a backpack or not even that, and flee to wherever it is still possible.

My father who, in spite of everything, was really and truly a very clever man but did not have enough imagination to envision the depth of human evil, thought a bit and said, 'I am able to understand this boy very well, and I am sure that in his short life he survived many horrible things.

'Even here, he is without identity papers and can be detained any second. He is in a foreign country, with people whose language he does not speak; he needs help, and is ready to tell anything, to get it. It goes without saying that we have to do everything in our power to help him, but that does not mean that we have to believe every word of his story. It is clear that terrible things are happening now to Jews in Poland, but factories of death in the middle of the twentieth century in the heart of Europe?!

'And how can you imagine that now, after their great defeat in Stalingrad, the Germans have enough trains at their disposal to drive Jewish families through the continent only to kill them. And what does he mean, with his advice to sell everything and flee? First of all, it is forbidden. Secondly, exactly which country is ready to accept you, or even allow you a transit? In these times to cross the well-guarded borders is possible, if at all, only with help from professional smugglers and must be very dangerous. And what about the sick, the aged, the babies, you are ready to leave them? And above all, we know that the Regent Miklos Horthy would never surrender the Hungarian Jews to the Germans.'

Azriel Feuerstein

Without doubt, there was something in what Father said. It was really impossible for such things to happen. And if it were true, the BBC would be full of it, day and night, threatening the criminals, warning the Jews to flee, and strongly protesting against the killings of innocents. It is true that here and there we heard about atrocities perpetrated against Jews, but it was only seldom and without details. In Yugoslavia there were partisans who fought against the Germans. There were no partisans in Kassa, although there are forests. But what would you do there, where would you sleep, what would you eat? And what was the hurry? In the meantime, there was nothing happening, and perhaps it wouldn't even come to that, as my father said. And if there is a German occupation of Hungary, and that is not probable because, after all, Hungary is Germany's ally in the war, then we would have to think about what to do.

One day, at the end of September 1943, somebody came into the store and told Father that Mother's older brother, Zoltan Altmann, wanted us to look him up in the evening. At that time there were no phones in private houses, and whenever somebody came to visit as a rule, he was welcomed, and that is why we found this request somewhat unusual. The whole day we tried to think about the cause of this invitation. We arrived. The evenings were getting colder at this time of the year. What could be so urgent? We rang the bell. After some waiting, Sari opened the door. We went upstairs and remained open mouthed, not believing our eyes. In the room Ilus' younger sister Klari, with her half-year old son Viki in her arms, who lived in Slovakia, welcomed us dressed in a Slovakian peasant's dress. Klari, as you remember, married Artur Sedlak without engagement(!). She tells us that the rumours about the deportations and the death-camps are now officially confirmed. After the wedding she and Artur went to live in Artur's village, Giraltovce, where nearly everyone, and everyone who mattered, was his close friend, and so he was told by the mayor and a gendarmerie officer separately that, within a week, the whole family would be deported. Artur sent Klari and Viki with a smuggler friend to Kassa, and he himself escaped to the Slovak partisans, that is if the Germans did not catch him.

We had to be practical. First of all Klari needed clothes and so did the baby. Viki needed food, and Zoltan and Sari couldn't go about buying baby food, as they would have been met with raised eyebrows. The whole thing had to be kept very secret since, if somebody was staying somewhere, even as a guest, for more than a few days, he had to register with the police. Father said that Mother should seek some of her own clothes for Klari and take the rest from the store, and find some of my baby clothes for Viki. As for baby food, Margit, Father's helper and right hand in the store, had a daughter of the same age, and she could be trusted blindly. Nobody should know about the guest, but if somebody should ask, then Klari was Sari's niece who came to visit for a few days. (Sari and her family were not Jews.) Sari deserves respect and many thanks for lying about Jews, which was not a small danger in those days, but then, she was very devoted to Zoltan, and anybody could see that there was a deeper bond between them than between a housekeeper and her employer.

On our way home we had quite a few thoughts and questions. To cross the border at night with a smuggler, and with a half-year old baby?! That was not only against the law, but very dangerous too. In addition, Klari was a foreign citizen. Could there perhaps be a way to get her and the child identity papers? Maybe things could be explained to the police? What if somebody informed the police about Sari and Zoltan? Moreover, if you think about it, we, ourselves, were accessories in crime. Anyway, how can a wife run away and leave her husband because of a rumour? They said that the family would be deported to Auschwitz, but how could they send a family with a baby to work? They were not officially told about the deportation. It was a rumour only. Perhaps they should have waited for a few days and not be so quick about fleeing? And living in the same house with Zoltan? Klari was a young woman and Zoltan, he was a widower. Nevertheless, what was really playing on our minds was *what was happening in that dark place they called Auschwitz?* And what was really happening in that Auschwitz? Our idiotic questions kept spinning like a cat running after its tail. The reality was too hard to face. But what is reality?

The next day we visited Zoltan again, with clothes and food for the baby. Viki was a very nice baby who did not weep much. There was a garden around the house and they slept in an inner room in the basement. So even if the baby cried, it could not be heard outside, but to be safe, if he cried, they turned the radio on. Viki smiled a lot and Sari fell in love with him. She played with the child and we spoke with Klari. She told us that in the last months, two boys had succeeded to escape from Auschwitz, with documents and plans of the camp.

Now we know how many camps there were in this compound, the precise place of the gas chambers, where the crematoriums were and how many ovens there were in each one. They said that the daily capacity for burning corpses was 2,500. They brought out the name of the camp commander, the list of the officers and the number of SS personnel. All that was confirmed from other sources as well. It was also known that Eastern Europe was then nearly empty of Jews, and that the deportations were going ahead at full speed, now from German occupied Western Europe too. We three sat around and didn't know what to say.

At this point Klari did something that could be called spreading panic and abusing her rights as a guest. 'Now listen to what I have to say', she said. 'I know that it is not easy to hear it, but you must. You, here in Hungary, are the last Jews in Europe who are living more or less in security, but you must understand that this seeming security is illusory and temporary. If nothing else, you have at least to do all the possible preparations for fleeing at a moment's notice and leaving everything behind.

'When the worst happens, it happens without warning. You have to slowly sell everything, buy diamonds and dollars if you can, things that don't weigh much and can be easily hidden. Houses and land you have to sell to Christians you can trust, and be ready to flee.

THE TUMBLER

'They say that for now the deportations from Rumania have ceased and perhaps you could hire somebody to take you there. The best would be to somehow get to Turkey, and from there to Palestine, it is no problem.

'You have to understand', she continued, 'that there is no point even in thinking about taking with you the old, the sick and the infirm unless you have a way to prepare a bunker, stock it with food for a long period, and a trustworthy Christian who is prepared to endanger himself and his family to hide you.' We sat there and looked at her as if she spoke Chinese.

'Hear me well', Klari continued with her monologue, 'there is no place there for sentiments. Everybody who is able to save himself has to do it and it is very important to know whom to trust. You have to know that the people who are going to help you, place themselves, their family, their property and their life in great danger. There will be a great temptation, even for the best among them, to inform on the Jews in hiding, and, thereby, get their property. I know', as Klari ended her speech, 'that I am speaking against my own interests, but you have to look at the reality with wide-open eyes.'

Things like that are not fit for human consumption, or as they say in Hungarian, 'not to swallow and not to spit out'. We were walking homewards, in our beloved hometown, our clothes and behaviour bearing witness to our respectable place in society. Here and there, acquaintances and friends greeted us, and Father responded by doffing his hat.

At the crossroad stood police officer Kovacs who greeted us with a smile and half-salute; his wife got special prices at the store and his unmarried daughter, who came in and presented herself as officer Kovacs's next of kin, got a special price too. One has to preserve good relations with the law. It was not easy to imagine that half the world wanted to kill us with gas and burn our bodies. Would this friendly officer Kovacs come to drive us out of our house, home and store? What would the neighbours say? Anyway, the whole thing could not last much longer; it was absolutely clear that Hitler was at the end of his rope. In Africa the Allied Forces had annihilated the great, glorious General Rommel and captured more prisoners of war than the Russians in Stalingrad. Sicily was occupied, Mussolini a prisoner, Italy would be surrendering in a few days, and the Russians had crossed the Dnepr, the third longest river in Europe. We were already in January 1944. How long could the war last? Surely, not long.

The Chanukah festivities were a bit late, as usual, to bring them closer to the Carnival. This year there wouldn't be a ball as many young men were in the Labour Service and instead of the dance there would be a festive evening with Leo Spielberg as the master of ceremonies. His dialogs were funny, his jokes a bit risqué for the grownups, but the younger set were very satisfied. All agreed that it was a very nice evening. We were in the sixth form of the high school so even if there had been a dance, we could not have participated since it was allowed only from the seventh form. We wouldn't miss it next year when all this trouble would be over.

The next Saturday we met at usual in Grandma's garden and everyone spoke about my approaching voyage. Everybody knew, and I said it untold times, that I saw my future in Palestine. Since Klari had come some half a year before, they didn't speak of rumours any more and accepted that horrible things were happening to Jews in all the lands around us; but perhaps it was not the right time? The war was going to end in the following days or months. In Hungary such horrible things were unimaginable, as everybody knew. This voyage should be thought about once more. Just for the sake of history, the date was 18 March 1944.

7

The Christian Neighbours and Deportation

'Hi, Yeory, what happened? Why don't you answer a friendly knock on the door? I hope that you didn't fall asleep on this sunny spring day?' asked Fröken Ulle.

'Welcome, Fröken Ulle. No, I really did not, but I was immersed in my thoughts, and you know, my hearing could be better. I walked around in the park before noon and enjoyed the fresh spring air. I see that you have my copybook. Were you possibly able to finish it?' I asked her.

'No, of course not. I only got to the date of 18 March 1944, that you specially mention,' replied Fröken Ulle.

'Yes, Fröken Ulle, the next day the Germans occupied Hungary and that was the gate of hell,' I woefully explained.

'Yeory,' said Fröken Ulle, 'on those pages where you describe the reaction of your family to the more and more alarming news about the fate of your relatives in Slovakia, how they are robbed of their property and sent one after the other to the supposed Death Camps, I feel a barely restrained rage and fury. What makes you so angry, and against whom is this rage directed?'

'Believe me, Fröken Ulle,' I replied, 'only against us and chiefly against myself. Not a single day goes by when I don't try to explain to myself the causes that made us so terribly blind. It is not the first and not the last time that I remember the Roman saying that "those the gods want to destroy, they make blind first", and there is no one as blind as somebody who voluntarily shuts his eyes and firmly refuses to see what is before his nose. It is true that all the Hungarian Jews were suffering from this self-inflicted blindness, but we, who had half our family gradually destroyed before our very eyes, forty kilometres away from us, who got a stream of news about brothers and uncles and sisters who were deported and killed, we, of all people, should not have succumbed to this comfortable and paralysing, self-inflicted blindness, this stupid unwillingness to see.

'This helpless, powerless impotence against the nearing catastrophe, this unwillingness to do something, anything, is more than I can understand and shall never forgive myself until the end of my life.'

'You see Yeory, I am very well able to understand your parents' behaviour. What they saw around them and heard about was so impossible to believe and realise, so against their expectations and against everything they knew about up to then that I don't wonder that they were immobilised, like a bird by a snake.

'But let's leave all that aside for a moment. Who are these two nice people in the picture[15]? While you tell me, I'll pour the coffee.'

As Fröken Ulle worked her charms on the coffee I explained, 'They are Ilus and her second husband Lada, after the war, but still in uniform. Ilus, if you remember, is a cousin, but she lived with us and I loved her like an older sister.

'Klari, who ran away from deportation in Slovakia, is her sister, and Ilus was the only one who did something about Klari's warning, got false papers as Christians for the both of them and, the day after the German occupation, she crossed the border into Slovakia and after much adventure and danger joined the partisans there.

'While with the partisans she met Lada, her second husband, who is not a Jew. Before the German occupation he was a pilot officer in the Czech Army and, as such, sent to a concentration camp from where he escaped and joined the partisans, who fought the Germans. There he became the leader of the group, Ilus became his secretary and they fell in love. After the war he returned to the Air Force as a career officer.'

Azriel Feuerstein

Fröken Ulle quizzed, 'Why did you especially remark that he is not a Jew? Is it so important? The main thing is that after so much suffering, they at last found happiness together.'

I agreed, 'You are right of course, Fröken Ulle, and I was really unable to understand her very religious brother, who, after they told him that his sister had married a non-Jew, mourned her as if she were dead.'

I did not tell her, and not even myself very much, that I, the great liberal and freethinker, when I visited them in Czechoslovakia, felt toward Ilus the old, unconditional love, like before the Holocaust, and was very happy to see her happiness and obvious love toward Lada, in whom she found her worthy and loving husband, but with whom I was... how shall I say it – uncomfortable.

I tried to tell myself that it was only because of the difficulties in communication – Lada spoke Czech, a language I don't speak well – but I have to confess that this feeling of strangeness had much deeper roots, roots that I was not proud of, and that in anyone else I would have found despicable.

I have to remark that Lada was an outstanding pilot, whom, after many years when the relations of the Soviet block with the Arab countries got friendly, his army wanted to promote him to general and send him to the Syrian Air Force as an instructor. He refused this promotion by saying that his wife is Jewish and had relatives in Israel, and he did not want to fight against them. He was very lucky as his courage did not cost him more than his career and they did not take his pension away.

Even before Ilus got sick with incurable muscle atrophy, Lada took care of her for more than twenty years with unflagging devotion and patience, like an angel. That only shows how wrong – and how deep - bigot prejudice is, even with us Jews who have suffered so long and so much from it and its consequences.

'And what happened to Klari?' Fröken Ulle asked.

'My Uncle Zoltan, in whose house she and her baby were hidden, despite all the warnings and tales that Klari told, went to the ghetto by himself as a law-abiding citizen. Sari, Zoltan's non-

Jewish housekeeper gave the baby to her cousin from a village for safekeeping and Klari fled to Budapest with Christian identity papers that Ilus had prepared for her. There she worked for a few months until the man from the Zionist underground she worked with was arrested, and there was grave danger that he would succumb to the torture and denounce the people he worked with.

'So Klari fled back to Kassa, one second before they were going to arrest her. There, some way, she found an empty, and for the moment, abandoned house without electricity, heating or running water – it was winter already. After some weeks a Hungarian policeman found her and saw at once that she was a hiding Jewish woman. So that he would not give her up to the police, she gave in to his extortion for money, and worse, and she had to fly back to Sari.

'This courageous and noble Christian woman took her in, despite the danger to her life, and despite the fact that there were two more Jewish families hidden there. Klari was liberated there, in Uncle Zoltan's house in January 1945, when the Russians liberated Kassa, now Košice, once again. She got her baby, Viki, back, her husband, Artur, returned from the partisans, and as I hear, they are preparing to emigrate to Palestine, too.'

'And tell me, Yeory, what about the neighbours, with whom you lived tens of years in friendship and mutual respect? They did not protest, they did not ask questions?'

'I asked these questions too and there are as many answers, as there are people. There were of course the rabid, ranting, bloodthirsty Jew-haters who denounced the hidden, were the willing and enthusiastic helpers of the murderers and cheered them on with shouts of joy; they were, shall we say, a minority.

'There was the great mass of the people who were neutral and indifferent, saying: "it is not our concern, it is the law of the country, and nobody asks for our opinion".

'There was a minority, and let's say at once, a small minority, who were concerned about the fate of the Jews, but they could not do anything. And there were the very, very few, whose numbers you could count on your fingers, who endangered themselves, their property and their family to save those who could be saved, like Sari for example. They are worthy of respect, gratefulness and can never be repaid.

'To understand all this better, let's remember a most important point: in our town of seventy thousand people at that time, there were some twelve thousand Jews or four thousand families. Every family had an apartment with furniture; many had stores, a shop, a house, and property. I don't want to say that everyone took part in the plundering as most belongings were taken by the gendarmerie, the police, the state and, of course, by the Germans, but something trickled down, anyway.

'There were good neighbours who got property, jewels, etc to keep safe until the Jews' return, and most of them intended to give it all back to the returning Jews; of course, they did. On the other hand, if it so happened that some of these poor families never came back, it would of course be very, very sad but...

'And let's not forget the many advocates, doctors, storekeepers, tailors, barbers, hairdressers, etc who inherited all the clients and customers of the so regrettably but so conveniently murdered ones. No, believe me, the returning Jews were certainly not greeted with shouts of joy.'

'Is that what you really believe, Yeory, that people are influenced by such material considerations only? Is money everything?

I quipped, 'That question reminds me of the widow, who, if only her husband returned, would gladly give back *half* of his life insurance.'

Fröken Ulle looked puzzled as she asked, 'What widow, Yeory, what are you talking about?'

I thought to myself, *OK, she is Swedish after all and understanding humorous remarks is not their strong point.*

'Let's leave all that for now', she said, changing the subject. 'Sit down and drink your coffee before it gets cold. I see from what you wrote how much you would like to return to those years before the deportation, which, as I understand, were very beautiful.'

THE TUMBLER

I replied with disdain in my voice, 'If it seemed so to you, I did something I really did not intend to. My childhood was happy, it is true, but is there a really happy teenager? Those years are always full of problems, uncertainty and self-doubt, and I, a shy, diffident and fat boy, had certainly my share of it and tormented myself enough. I told myself then that when, in later years, somebody would try to recall these years as the happiest in my life, as it sometimes happens in books that are written by old men with short memories, I'd spit him in the eye.'

'What you say, Yeory, is very true, and believe me, for girls it is even harder. Those years as a teenager are a difficult time in life and their problems seem so small only when seen through the rosy veil of memories. I see that you got your appetite back, at lunch you did not eat anything.'

'I'll tell you something, but, please, let it remain between us: there are a lot of things I don't eat. I don't talk about food I don't like, or don't prefer; simply there are things I am unable to taste, and in fact I never did like tomatoes, cucumbers, prunes and so on. But what I really and truly hate is what we had today, sauerkraut.'

'You should have grown up in my family. We had to remain sitting at the table until we had finished the food on our plate.'

'That was tried in my family too. We made our sauerkraut at home. In the basement there was a big barrel for that purpose. The cabbage was hobbled into it, my father rolled up the legs of his pants, took me on his shoulder, stepped into the barrel and commenced to dance in it, to the great merriment of all, and mine too, in order to bring up the juice of the cabbage. After that they put in sour apples, whole black peppers, bay leaves, covered it and on the cover they put some heavy stones to press it down.

'Up till then, I had no quarrel with the whole procedure and, sitting on Father's shoulders, I even enjoyed it; but after that, when the damned mixture began to stink to high heaven of sauerkraut, I did not even go near the basement. The whole situation was complicated by the fact that my father could not live without it; it was served to him with the meat every Saturday and

70

some days after that too. He did not like me being so choosy about food, but I could not abide, wouldn't even taste, sauerkraut.

'One day, when I was about nine years old, he sat me on his knee asked the maid to serve me a small plate of sauerkraut and potato and made me eat it while I was in tears. In the evening I was running a forty-degree fever. The doctor came and said that I had scarlatina (also called scarlet fever), a dangerous illness at that time, and they put a red warning on the door that put me out of bounds for three weeks and I did not go to school. It is very probable that it had nothing to do with eating sauerkraut, but one thing is certain, never again did they force me to eat things I did not like.'

Fröken Ulle's parting words were, 'What shall I say, Yeory, it seems, that you were a bad lot even then! It is pretty late and I have to go. I am taking your copybook with me and I'll see you tomorrow.'

'See you soon, Fröken Ulle, and thanks for everything.'

8

The German Occupation

Sunday, 19 March 1944. The Germans occupy Hungary to 'secure their lines of supply' with the full cooperation of the Hungarian Army. The next day, going to school, we see three smiling German soldiers with heavy machineguns on every street corner. The people on the street are smiling too. After two hours of hanging about, we are sent home and the Germans occupy the school. It is an annoyingly beautiful spring day, with a festive air in the town and Main Street is full of people. From time to time, specially selected German units march along, singing. In every troop there are some whistlers who accompany the singing and give a solo once in a while, which really sounds very good. They get applauded too. Here and there, some people raise their arm in a Hitler-salute. People look musingly at the Jewish stores. In the evenings some neighbours and 'good friends' come to visit and, after some casual conversation, they offer to take care of our property, 'if you should have to leave, God forbid'.

On the walls there appear new announcements every day. The Jews have to hand in radios, gold, jewels. The Jews are forbidden to employ non-Jewish domestics, so we have to let Marish go, who had been with us for more than ten years. The Jewish bank accounts are closed. My father had a way with the bank: he was the director's good friend and a special client. With her marriage, Mother had inherited a dinner service of solid silver, complete for twenty-four persons which, in its velvet-lined box, weighed more than twenty kilograms. My father put it in the bank, as a security for a loan he took for a year. Before Pesach we brought the box home and Mother and Marish cleaned the silver for a week.

THE TUMBLER

Father paid back the loan and the interest he paid was less than he would have paid for keeping the silver for a year in the bank's vaults. This year, the box came home some days before the Germans arrived. Father had not paid the loan back yet so we gave the box for safekeeping to a 'secure' Christian neighbour and friend, and we had enough money at home. It was necessary to think about the rest of the property, but we were lucky: this same Christian neighbour, by the name of Gazsik, had a store next to ours with his Jewish partner Kertesz Mano, and there we hid some boxes with private property as well as some of the goods from the store. Now, if the worst were to happen, Gazsik would keep them for us until we returned. After the war, when I came back from Sweden for a visit to Kassa, I found Gazsik in our store, which was much bigger than theirs. When he saw me, he nearly fell down and explained with deep sorrow that the goods and boxes the Germans took, the silver was stolen by the Russians, and 'all these goods are new'. But he was, I think, even sorrier, because the store, its furniture and some fixtures, were undeniably ours.

6 April 1944. Every Jew has to wear the yellow star. It is not very pleasant, but today we have to go to school to get the record-card as the school year is over. Instead of the anticipated mockery, there are some in the street who greet us first, and some who turn their head, not wanting to notice the yellow star. In the school, the situation is the same. The most pitiful are those who were born as Christians, because although their parents had converted to Christianity now they have to wear the yellow star because of the racial laws. They are not able to look into the eyes of neither the Jews nor the Christians. My report card is worse than anticipated, and so are the report cards of the rest of the Jews. The head of the class says that the circumstances, you know... Who cares? On the way home, I see my friend and classmate, Nussenzweig Ervin, cycling down Main Street, without the yellow star, towards the forest. He made it to the partisans and survived. Such a thing warms my heart when I tell about these things.

74

Azriel Feuerstein

Saturday, 14 April. As usual, we meet in the grandparents' garden. Everybody knows that it is the last time we would meet before the war ends. Nobody imagines that it would be our last meeting and that I would be the only one to survive. As usual, there are five families there: Grandma and Grandpa, Father's sisters, Schapira Manyi and her little daughter, Goldberg Aliz and her two daughters, Boehm Elek and his daughter Zsuzsika, Father, Mother and I. Everybody has brought something to hide, that, above its real value, has some sentimental value too. You cannot hide everything because you have to leave something for them to confiscate, so as not to be tortured, and some valuables we hope to take with us, sewn in our clothing. Take with us…where?

My father takes the things we decided to hide and disappears for a good while together with Boehm Elek. When they return, Father is satisfied. 'You can be sure that they will have to tear down the house to find them', he says. I believe him; he has, as his son does not, golden hands. The grandparents and Father's sisters go with him as he wants to show them where the things are hidden. 'Take Gyurika with you', says Mother, but Father is superstitious, and says that when we return, we shall take it out together. It was not to be. When I, the only survivor, returned home for a visit two years after the war, I had no idea where even to begin to look.

In three days I would have my sixteenth birthday, and I feel bad that nobody remembered and wished me many happy returns.

There follows a hectic week. The Jews are taken to the ghetto, that is, to the brickyard. A policeman comes and says that in two hours we have to be ready and that everyone can take one suitcase. You have to hand over the keys of the apartment and the wardrobes and they will take you with all the packages to the other side of the town.

Saturday evening. Someone is knocking. It is police officer Kovacs in civilian clothing. You can see that he is nervous, awkward and performing an unpleasant task. He tells us that he has an order to come tomorrow, together with an official from the

75

tax authorities, to take us to the brickyard. 'You are allowed only one suitcase per person, but if there are one or two more, they will close their eyes.' He reminds us to take warm clothes and cover because the nights are cold and windy. He tells us that he took the liberty to speak with a coachman to come tomorrow to take us so that we won't have trouble with the packages on the long way to the brickyard. Then he tells us that he is sorry, but tomorrow he will have to talk to us with disrespect, but, you know, these troubled times... My father thanks him sincerely because he really did us a great favour at some personal risk. Father gives him some money but Kovacs is reluctant to take it, saying that he does not do this for money, and promises to give it to the official he'll come with. Father understands the hint and gives him some more, for the official too.

We take out the suitcases and the rucksacks. We are lucky that we are used to walking so that everybody has one, as well as sturdy shoes and suitable clothing. Instead of pyjamas we'll take ski pants and warm underclothes, instead of bed sheets we'll take blankets. Some weeks ago I got my yearly new orthopaedic shoes for walking – I have flat feet – and Father says that we'll have to scratch them some so they do not take them away. What about Mother's pictures and my books? Mother may take some, and I take the poems of Ady. A big jar of goose fat we jam in a rucksack and put clothes around it. If they take it away, so be it. At midnight everything is finished. Everybody has a rucksack and we have five suitcases too. If they say that it is too much, we'll leave some. We leave all the keys on the table: the keys of the store and the basement too. At last Mother puts everything in its place, closes the wardrobes and the cupboards, and washes the windows and the floor otherwise 'what will they think of us?'

Next day is Sunday, 23 April 1944, one month and three days after the German occupation. At ten o'clock there is a knock on the door. It is Kovacs in his uniform and with a threatening face. The official accompanying him sees that we are ready and asks how we knew that they were coming. Father explains that the Jewish council told us. We beg them to take any keepsakes they fancy. They do us the favour. We give them the keys. They close the doors and put on them and on the windows a broad red band proclaiming 'Jewish property. Seized by the state'. Kovacs and the other man help us to take the packages down to the gate. From there the waiting coachman helps to load them on the carriage.

The sun is shining. It is a glorious spring day. The prayer in the churches is finished and Main Street is full of passers-by. The 'korzo' is in full swing, as usual; of course, without the Jews now, but you don't see the difference. Some smile mockingly at the carriages, laden with Jews – ours isn't the only one – taking them, who knows where. Here and there you even hear some derogatory remarks, chiefly from the rabble, whose place is not usually on the 'korzo', but who now proudly swagger around, with their brand-new arrow-cross badge on their breast. They are not encouraged. I see some of my Christian classmates. We turn our heads, embarrassed. What hurts most is that there is almost no change. You can't see that every seventh citizen was torn out of the life of the town. The carriage ambles around slowly, and Main Street seems endless. We turn down Szepesi Street. There is no other way to the brickyard. However unpleasant and embarrassing this may be, Kovacs deserved every penny he got for ensuring the coach so that we didn't have to do it by foot.

We arrive at the gate of the brickyard. The police at the gate want us to load off the suitcases and take them ourselves all the way in. Kovacs speaks with them, and they allow us to take them in by carriage. Not too far away from the huge brick drying sheds, two cock-feathered gendarmes stop us and we have to load off everything, say goodbye and thanks to Kovacs. Some friends see us and they come to help us to take the packages up to the sheds.

A highway and a railroad, by which the bricks were transported, divided the brickyard. In both parts there were these huge brick drying sheds. These sheds had of course no walls so that the wind could dry the bricks better. The high roof rested on a timber framework with beams every four metres. We were the first ones to arrive at 'our' shed and occupied a corner. Mother stuck into one package a broom without handle, but it took me only a moment to find a handle in all the debris around and we cleaned our corner, more or less. Under Father's directions we gathered a big pile of broken bricks and built a one and half-metre high wall as defence against the wind and rain, spread rugs and blankets on the floor, and defined our corner with our suitcases around it. There were many envious eyes around us so we decided that somebody should always stay there to keep an eye on the things, and to hold both sides near us for friends. Boehm Elek and his family arrived within a few hours and we all felt more secure. It all happened in the last days of April and the first days of May, so it stands to reason that there were many days of rain, but I don't remember ever getting wet because we were too busy.

We had to keep up some semblance of order near the few water taps, near the kitchen. We had to dig ditches for the latrines, one for the women and one for the men. We did not get any help, of course, from the command of the Ghetto; quite the contrary. They did not allow any covering of the backside of the latrines facing the rampart which surrounded the brickyard, where the gendarmes patrolled, who whiled away a good part of their time on the rampart behind the women's latrine.

There was a big problem with food. Here in the brickyard we were together with Jews from the surrounding villages, who were driven out of their homes and had to take whatever they could by hand and had had to walk. Moreover, this was on the last day of Pesach when there was no bread at home, and, besides, they did not know what to take first: some clothing or food their many children. The Jewish Council did its best, and they organised a kitchen within a few hours, but food was a problem. This is where the Zionist Youth, or rather Offner Robert, known as Fifi, who was some two or three years above me in school, played an important role. With great energy, courage, bribery and not a little 'chuzpa', he made the command of the Ghetto accept the idea that a group of young students, accompanied by policemen, should visit the abandoned richer Jewish houses, take the food from their pantries and bring it to the brickyard. So we went out, a group of some fifty youths wearing the yellow star, through the town, with policemen in military formation, and emptied the pantries. That did not only bring in some food, but the policemen were not left empty-handed either. Here I am somewhat hazy. What I know is that Fifi managed to get forged papers and escaped to Budapest. It seems that it was arranged before, because everyday somebody did the same and when we arrived in the evening, nobody counted us. I told father that one of these days I too would get false papers and he only said that he'd hide some money in my shoes and toothpaste.

One day they came and told me that I had got my papers and could escape. The problem was that I was wearing another coat and not the one that was specially prepared so that I could take the yellow star off easily, and I did not have the money with me. I did not want to leave without saying goodbye to my parents either. 'It does not matter. I'll do it on Monday.' That was on Saturday, 13 May 1944.

We get to the brickyard and see that there is a lot of running around. There is a new group of gendarmes. They close the gates. Here I must explain that at that time in Hungary there were two bodies responsible for keeping the peace. There were the blue-uniformed urban policemen, armed with a handgun and a nightstick, who were responsible for the towns; and there was the gendarmerie, in military uniforms with cock-feathered black hats, who always walked around in pairs, with rifles with ninety centimetre long fixed bayonets on them. They were responsible for the villages and were known as bloodthirsty beasts. Their chief duty was to intimidate and terrify. It was clear that, if they were commandeered here, it could mean nothing good.

Monday, 15 May 1944, fifty-seven days after the German occupation. The suitcases are repacked. Mother prepares a canteen of water. Father tells me in secret that everyone has two tubes of 'toothpaste', but not to open them when anyone is near because there is money in them. In every coat, there is some jewel or money sewn in. We get to the gate before the wagons where there are two gendarmes with a big basket, enjoying themselves and demanding the engagement rings and the earrings too. After all those years, they don't come off easily. One of the gendarmes wants to amuse himself and tells a young woman to take off her blouse because he wants to see if she does not have a necklace hidden there. At the last moment an SS officer, who is observing from the side, tells the police officer to replace the two gendarmes with policemen to speed up the process.

We get to the railway. It is a freight train, with closed cattle wagons; in every wagon there is a small opening, a 'window' closed with barbed wire for ventilation. On every wagon there is an inscription: *8 horses or 20 soldiers.*

Around the wagons there are policemen, gendarmes, armed soldiers and a few SS men who push people without mercy and without end into the wagons. We see that it is better not to be the last one, climb onto an empty wagon and occupy the corner at the far end from the window. That is what Father wanted and he knew why. It seems that the wagon is full already, but it is not enough for these beasts in human shape. With hands, truncheons, rifles, they force in more and more. Shouting and crying. People tread on each other. There is no place for the packages. There is barely place for standing. At last they push in one bucket of water and an empty one for the needs of some eighty people. They close the door with deafening noise, chain it from the outside and seal it with a lead stamp of the SS. The train stands there in the hot May sun. The women swoon. The children seek their parents and in this hell there is no need for devils, the lost souls torment each other and themselves with their own hands in their hard packed misery.

After the war, I read the story of the deportations. Our train was the third one after the trains from Munkács and Nyiregyháza. Between 14 May and 21 June 1944, in just 41 days, 137 such trains passed the Kassa Railway Station, with more than 3,000 tormented souls per train, or exactly – the Germans were nothing if not exact – 394,156 persons. And these are only the trains through Kassa, towards Auschwitz. Some 25,000 were sent to Austria, many more were led there in Death Marches, the blood of many more painted red the half-frozen waters of the Danube and many thousands more of the flower of Jewish youth were tortured and worked to death in the 'military' Labour Service. In making our reckoning with Hungary it is important to understand that, in the published statistics after the war, these numbers were divided between Rumania, Czechoslovakia, Yugoslavia, and Ukraine as at the time part of those territories were included in Hungary. These Jews spoke of themselves as Hungarian Jews who were sent to the slaughterhouse by the Hungarian government, under the leadership of Admiral Miklos Horthy who, for some reason, was thought and spoken of even by Jews as a kind of saint. However shameful, and no matter how much it hurts all concerned, there is another fact that has to be mentioned: all these 137 trains running through Kassa, that took four hundred thousand babies, children, women and men to their death, less than one year before the end of war, had to make their way through a railway tunnel one-and-a-half kilometres after Kassa. One bombing strike against it, of which there were thousands daily at that time, would have been sufficient to put it out of action and stop or delay the deportations.

In the early hours of the afternoon our train began to move at last. The bucket of water was empty already and the other one full. There was a small opening between the closed door and the wagon and the men peed through it, but it did not help much. The urine, and more, spilt over and spread around. Luckily, we were far away. There was no way to avoid it, and somehow they made an opening wider in the wire that closed the window and the disgusting overflow made its way in some kind of vessel from hand to hand all the way to the window where they poured it out. They tried to do it in such a way that half of it should not be blown back and in the packed wagon, and that was neither easy nor nice. I don't want to go into detail about what happened to the rest, but all this, the inhuman conditions, the disgust and the shame, had their well-planned purpose: to crush and destroy individuality and self-respect.

After some twenty minutes the train went through the tunnel and we understood that we were going eastwards, toward Poland.

THE TUMBLER

Shouting, crying, hysteria. Somebody dies in the middle of the wagon and the family shouts for a doctor. There is no doctor, but even if there was, how could he help? They fasten the dead man, standing up, near the window for more space. After some two hours the train stops to let other and more important trains pass. We shout and beg them to open the door, to empty the full bucket. There is no answer. In the evening, when the train stops again, they open the door at last, to empty the bucket of waste. During the whole journey of 57 hours, it was the only opportunity to do it. There is no water to rinse it. Luckily there is some wet grass. The dead men – there is another one in the meantime – have to remain in the wagon. In the night the train stops again, and somebody beats on the side of the wagon, and shouts, 'Ihr werdet alle erschossen.' (You will all be shot.) What is this ridicule and gloating, or perhaps, warning? Father tries to be optimistic, as always.

'They haul us through half of Europe to kill us? That is not logical.' To tell the truth, there is not much logic in all this life. Father embraces Mother to calm her down and Zsuzsika and I snuggle together there in the darkness, the first and last time ever.

The first light of dawn separates us. It is Wednesday, and we haven't arrived yet. Everybody is very thirsty but we have a mouthful of water left, thanks to Mother's foresight. We give some to Elek, and make sure that nobody sees us. They say that there are five dead already, two of whom poisoned themselves.

Everything has to come to an end eventually, and so does this journey. The train slows down. It is evening. Those who stand near the window say that we have stopped before a huge camp. There is a great hullabaloo around. We hear the rattle of chains, the clang of the doors of neighbouring wagons being opened. The door of our wagon crashes open too. In the door stands a man, clad in blue-white stripped pyjama-like clothes and a service cap who shouts at the top of his voice, like everyone else around, 'Los, los, alle heraus!', which means everyone out, at once, leave everything in the wagon, even the coats! I ask him, in Hebrew, where were we, and he whispers, 'Auschwitz. Everybody young,

everybody healthy!', and throws out the people who hesitate in
the door.

Auschwitz?! That is a name I had heard before. There is not
much time for thinking. It had been raining here not so long ago.
The asphalt of the wet, wide platform reflects the light of the high
lighting-poles. The row of armed SS men competes in howling
with their dogs they hold on leashes. A lot of pyjama-clad
prisoners, with the usual shouting and beating, move the people
away from the wagons, throw out the dead and those who are
unable to move, and push everyone, the dead and the living, onto
the lorries parked nearby. Big well-fed men, clad in better
pyjamas and with 'Capo' inscribed on red armbands, armed with
metre-long rubber hoses beat everyone and separate men from
women. My mother was some steps away from us, but a group of
women dragged her with them, away from us and we could not
even kiss her goodbye. Father and I are thrown into a long line
that moves slowly forward. We see that the line arrives before a
shining black booted SS officer with eyeglasses and white gloves
and a short stick in his hands. After him the line divides into two:
the majority goes to the left and some people to his right side. My
father is before me. The SS asks him: 'Wie alt?' that is, 'how old
are you?' 'Fünfzig', fifty, he answers, for some reason. He was
only forty-eight. Why did he say more? Perhaps he believed in his
optimism? Who knows? They took him to the left side. I wanted
to follow him, but the capo near the officer threw me to the right.
To this very day I don't know if I should be thankful to him, or
hate him.

Those of us directed towards the right were lined up in threes
with much shooting and beating. I was in the first row, at the
platform's edge. Suddenly, we see a group of older women and
women with children nearing the road, under the platform. In the
first row I see my mother supported on both sides by two friends.
She too becomes aware of me. And out of the throat of this
reticent, soft-spoken woman, who I don't remember ever raising
her voice, breaks out a terrible, desperate, piercingly loud,
howling shout: 'GYURIKA!!!'

THE TUMBLER

It seemed that in all that noise, commotion, racket and tumult, for a second there was silence and my mother's voice cut in two the boiling hell around us, and cut my life too in two unequal parts, two parts that will never be able to unite and knit together.

9

The Unwillingness to See

The eyes of Fröken Ulle were red from crying.

'Forgive me, I wanted to finish the first part of your story and that is why I am late,' she said, when she came in.

'I was reading the poems of Gustav Fröding, much happier reading material than what you had to struggle with, and perhaps even written with more talent,' I replied, jokingly.

'Written with more talent? This unexpected modesty surprises me. Anyway, you made me cry,' explained Fröken Ulle

'Yes, I see it from your red eyes and I am really sorry that, beside the work of making coffee and cookies, I had to trouble you with the tragic fate of a strange, far away people,' I consoled.

'Let nobody say that Fröken Ulle does not understand delicate hints. Sit down, and let's drink first. But, to say the truth, I understood that it was our conversations you awaited so impatiently,' she said with a warm smile.

'The important thing is, Fröken Ulle, that I made you smile. Believe me, our conversations are not less important to me than the coffee, and considering how tasty your cookies are, that is no small compliment. But tell me, did you not stop to ask yourself, strictly speaking, what I have got to do with all this? Is it possible that the persecution of Jews had no reason at all? And what concern is all this to you Swedes?' I asked,

'See here, Yeory, I would lie to you if I said that no such questions were asked here, chiefly during the war, when the Holocaust and its terrible results were not yet known, and were thought by many as no more than propaganda by the Allies, or unimaginable exaggerations. You could hear such opinions when

THE TUMBLER

the Norwegian and Danish undergrounds saved the Jews in their own country and brought them here by boats illegally, but with the consent of the Swedish government. There were not a few who asked what concern of ours is all this? Why do we, in neutral Sweden, have to enter into conflict with one side, the Germans who are on their way to win the war? Why do we have to endanger our neutrality for the sake of a few Jews, who are not even our citizens? Isn't it clear that, if the Germans wanted to, they would be able to occupy Sweden, as they did the rest of Scandinavia? I want to say that I am proud of my country for not thinking twice about helping the persecuted,' said a proud Fröken Ulle.

She was proud, with a good reason. Her country did more for the persecuted Jews, than nearly every other nation. Then, when there was a danger in it, when the empire of the evil was at the summit of its power, Sweden, with the help of the Norwegian and the Danish underground rescued a good part of those countries' Jews and took them into their land, in the middle of the war, when the doors of all other countries were firmly shut, and in accepting them, there was no small danger.

'You know, Fröken Ulle, I often ask myself, why? Why did Sweden have to put its neutrality in danger by opening its gates to these persecuted people at a time when every other country firmly closed its borders before the Jews? Why did they accept that they were fleeing before a fate that was worse than death? And at a time when we, who were sitting on the volcano's top, were unable to believe it?' I asked with impassion.

Fröken Ulle replied, 'I think that it was the Scandinavian solidarity, chiefly. We said to ourselves that if the Norwegians and the Danes endangered their lives to save their Jews, we too had to do everything possible. Say, Yeory, if you knew what had happened in neighbouring countries, and you even knew the fate of your relatives not far away from you, you must have realised the same fate awaited you in case of German occupation. Had you no way to organise some kind of resistance for if and when it occurred?'

Azriel Feuerstein

I replied, 'Believe me, I have tortured myself with this question, ever since Klari came with her baby, and cannot find the answer. There were two possible directions for action: individual or organised. The first option meant that you accepted that everybody who could, had to save himself as best he could and the devil take the hindmost. It is true that my presence would not have helped my parents anyway, as it did not, but I don't know how I could have looked at myself in the mirror if I had left them of my own free will. It is more difficult to explain why there was no preparation for organised resistance. It is a fact that the community and the Zionist organisations helped the Jewish refugees: they got some money and advice about where to get false papers. Why could not such a thing have been prepared on a larger scale for the Hungarian Jews themselves? The answer is that the leadership, like the masses, could have no idea that such things would happen.

'I know that it sounds like a kind of sick joke, but even when we were in Auschwitz, with its chimneys and the smell, and heard about the gas chambers, even then we still talked about meeting our parents after the war. But I digress. The leadership did nothing to prepare us for when we came under German occupation because they wanted to adhere to legality, and they did not want to create a panic which, in their opinion, would only have made the situation worse.'

'And why do you think that there were no partisans like elsewhere?' asked Fröken Ulle.

I answered, 'In addition to the reasons I talked about before, such as the fear of mass panic, there were objective reasons too. The men aged twenty to forty were in the Labour Service, without military training. Those, with military training from the First World War, were by then over fifty. It was very difficult to lay your hands on weapons or explosives. Not only borders isolated us, but also fighting fronts which were nearly impossible to cross. We were isolated from the Jews of the world, who themselves were acting at cross-purposes. And the main reason: Mao Tsetung said that the underground fighter has to immerge himself

87

into the masses of his people who shield him. But the Jewish fighter had no such privilege. The very masses of his people were condemned to death, unlike the Chinese or French.

'The Jewish resistance, if and when it existed, could not for a moment operate under its own name because that would have antagonised not only the Germans but also other nations that had different aspirations from the Jewish fighter. Jews took part in the Yugoslav, French and Slovak movements and in the fighting armies against Hitler in numbers far exceeding their proportion in the population, but they had to do it as Yugoslav, French, Slovak citizens who fought for independence only, at the time when the Jews were fighting for their right to exist.

'After having said all that, and all we said is true, we have to look in the mirror and admit that the Holocaust was so big because heroism was so small. Perhaps not too small if we take into consideration all that we said before, but too small under the circumstances. That, we have to remember. We are used to speaking of and remembering the Holocaust and heroism. There is some solace in that. There was the Holocaust, but there was heroism too. We should not let ourselves forget that the Holocaust was so vast, so huge, so unimaginable also because heroism was so small, compared to it.'

'Don't you think, Yeory,' asked Fröken Ulle, 'that by saying that you offend the feelings of a whole generation? Isn't there a kind of holiness in that they went to their fate with submission and accepted their martyrdom with obedience? Are we allowed to criticise, or perhaps even accuse them, instead of revere their sacred memory with bowed head and tears in our eyes?'

'That is true, Fröken Ulle. There is a saying in all languages that there should be nothing bad said of the dead, and it should be so, but I belong to this generation and it is only a quirk of fate that my name is not on one of the many memorial plates. So I am allowed to protest that my generation went so obediently to the slaughterhouse. We should not accept it and not educate in this spirit, we should not accept the unacceptable as God's will and see in it something saintly. Our Wise Men said that if somebody meets many misfortunes, one after the other, he should examine his deeds to find out why this is happening to him and where he erred? That is what the Jews should do, whose history since the Second Temple was destroyed in an unbroken chain of pogroms, persecutions, charges of ritual murders, deportations, rapes, scorn, hate and loathing, up to this very day.

'There was a time when the Wise Men said that God showed his mercy by dispersing his people all over the world. When persecuted in one country, they'll thrive in another. But the Holocaust showed us that the world is getting smaller. There was a time when we thought that assimilation, the age of enlightenment, liberalism, and socialism would bring a change, but it was not to be. Neither dispersion nor emigration helped; wherever the Jew went, hate followed. It did not help when he tried to be like the people around him in language, apparel, speech, and behaviour. He went so far as believing that he was no different, but was always painfully reminded by his surroundings.

'The enlightenment, the culture, the science did not help: they only made the instruments of murder more efficient. The ideas of socialism and equality did not help: we were always less equal. They will always hate and persecute the weak and the different. If you don't believe me, Fröken Ulle, just see what happens to a wounded hen in her roost: she gets pecked to death by the other hens. That is why we Jews should understand that we must stop being dispersed or else the Diaspora will eliminate us, and that is why my way leads to Palestine.'

'We are people, Yeory, not hens! We are able to see what we have done and change our ways. Now that we have seen where anti-Semitism leads the world, no nation will allow it to spread. The first ones to denounce it with loathing will be the Germans. Today they are ashamed to look other nations in the eye. Concerning Palestine, there are a few problems there too, I understand. Don't you think that this kind of concentration of the Jews is what the Nazis really wanted?'

'Human memory, chiefly about unpleasant issues, is limited. In a few years, there'll be learned debates about the number of Jews killed, and in which way they were responsible for it. Jews have the right and duty to live in their own land and solve their own problems in Palestine,' I replied.

'My problem and duty just now is that it is too late. See you tomorrow.'

'Fröken Ulle, thanks for everything, and goodbye.'

10

A Picture Says a Thousand Words

The images given reference numbers in the text can be seen in the plate section. They are each numbered to help you match them to the reference numbers given throughout the text.

(1) My maternal grandparents.

(2) Grandfather's obituary.

(3) My German nurse, Irma, and my father to my right.

(4) My parents and I (aged 6) before our trip to Budapest.

(5) *Left*, I am two years old walking in Kassa with my father in his urban fur coat.

(6) *Right*, with my father in my grandparents' garden.

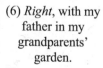

Azriel Feuerstein

(7) Our store. Standing in the door are Father, Mr Huebsch, the bookkeeper, and Margit the shop assistant. Marcsa is sitting in the forefront, at the edge of the sidewalk, selling flowers.

(8) *Left*, Grandfather (9) *Right*, Uncle Henrik Schapira, my mother and I, Henrik's son Gusti, my father's younger sister Manyi, and Grandma.

 (10) *Left*, Mother and I are at Lake Balaton, and on the back of the picture my mother wrote that it was after my tonsillectomy. (11) *Right*, Mother in the garden with the roses.

(12) Me, Father and Zsuzsika, Elek Boehm's daughter, in a brook

(13) Father's brother Rudi Dusika, and Father.

(14) This picture was taken when I was two years old and I am not in it. Here is Izso, the son of Erna and Zoltan Altmann, mother's older brother and Laci, a cousin, Alize Goldberg, father's older sister and her two daughters, Marta and Kato, Manyi, father's younger sister, and my parents.

Grandma's house.

Klari, with son Viki.

Azriel Feuerstein

Dora Krauss, *right*, another one of mother's older sisters, and her husband, Armin, *left*, were the owners of the tavern, the hotel and the whole family compound. Dora died in Slovakia, in the course of her deportation and was buried in Zilina in 1942. Her husband, Armin, their son, Philip, his wife Irina and their three-month-old daughter were deported and killed and my mother was unable to stop weeping.

(15) My cousin Ilus and her second husband Lada,
after the war, but still in uniform.

THE TUMBLER

Lilly, Ancsi and I. Ancsi and Lilly, the younger sisters of Ilus and Klari, were taken to the railway station and their hair shorn off. They were clothed in thin, blue and white striped pyjamas and taken away to…Auschwitz!

I as a librarian in Gothenburg.

Azriel Feuerstein

Annie and I married in 1948.

In 2002 the whole family went on a two-week 'shorashim' (seeking the roots) trip. From left to right: Dorit Gazit (Yehuda's wife), her daughter Gilly, Efrat Sonnenschein, Doron Gazit, me and Annie bursting with pride, our daughter Esther Sonnenschein, our son Yehuda Gazit with his daughter and our granddaughter Roni. From left to right, *sitting*: Nadav and Roni Sonnenschein.

THE TUMBLER

Dr Mengele cut a dashing figure in Nazi uniform. His horror experiments on inmates at Auschwitz earned him the sobriquet of 'The Angel of Death'.

Some females at Auschwitz actually called him a 'beautiful person'.

His experiments on twins were notorious, he once had twin boys killed so that he could settle an argument with another doctor! He slipped away just before Auschwitz was liberated!

This was the fate for many concentration camp Jews, to end up dead on a trolley, little dignity if any was granted at these times to those that passed away because of starvation.

Azriel Feuerstein

Lieutenant Colonel Ed F Soillor of the US Army stands amongst hundreds of Jewish prisoners burnt alive. Here he speaks to the German civilians he ordered to tour the ghastly camp. Although this image is from Landsberg Death Camp, this is what went on at many of the camps that were liberated by the American and English soldiers.

Nazi horror camp at Belsen. When the 11th Armoured Division of the British Second Army reached the Belsen camp, in Hanover, Germany, in April 1945 about 60,000 helpless Jews and political prisoners were found dying from starvation, typhus, typhoid and dysentery. Some had never had water for more than six days. The area was littered with decomposing bodies and investigation revealed that huts capable of sheltering 30 people were occupied by as many as 500. In many cases, prisoners had died of suffocation because they were too weak to struggle for a gasp of air.

THE TUMBLER

German prisoners of war are forced to exhume bodies of slave labourers. Here are some 800 bodies exhumed from a mass grave on the orders of American military authorities. When they were unable to complete a forced march from Buchenwald Concentration Camp they were murdered by SS troops. Location: five miles west of Passau, Germany. Date 15 May 1945.

Some camps were specifically equipped for mass killing by means of gas chambers and crematoria for disposing of the remains.

In the earlier camps some of the extermination methods were rather crude when exhaust fumes from truck engines or tank engines were pumped into sealed gassing vans, sealed railroad cars or specially constructed gas chambers.

In some of the later camps Zyklon-B pellets were used and in Stutthof lethal injections were used to kill sick prisoners. None of these methods made shootings, hangings and fatal beatings obsolete!

Two precedents for the death camps are the Nazi Euthanasia Project and the Aschaffenburg Concentration Camp.

A dead baby and the body of other children lie in the mass grave dug by German civilians of Nordhausen.

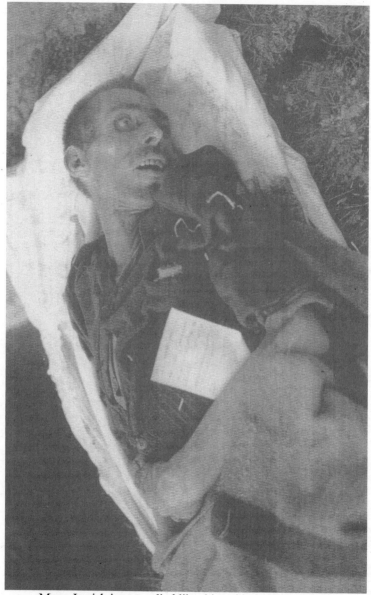

Many Jewish inmates died like this, with their eyes open.

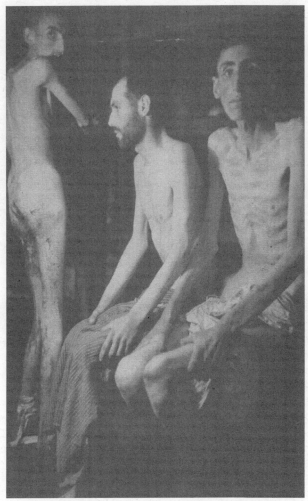

What can words say?

THE TUMBLER

Dachau – Liberation for prisoners from the horror camp of the Nazis, some wearing the characteristic striped dress of the concentration camp. They wildly cheer troops of the Seventh US Army. Note the hats being thrown/waived in the air.

An estimated 6 million Jews were murdered in the Holocaust. Over half were systematically exterminated by use of the gas chamber/crematorium system of the Nazi Death Camps between 1942 and 1945.

Treblinka, Auschwitz-Birkenau, Dachau, Chelmno, Sobibor, Belzek and Majdanek are names that will not be forgotten.

The Wannsee Conference, in Berlin, on 20 January 1942 the 'Final Solution' was an official policy and a major obsession of the Nazi regime. From this point onwards camps were constructed for the express purpose of radical mass extermination, principally of Jews, but of other groups as well.

Part Two

11

Auschwitz

Auschwitz. Here is the inscription above the gate: 'Arbeit Macht Frei' ('Work shall make you free'). The double electric fence with watchtowers and guards looked threatening. There is a strange smell in the air. Something is burning. The huge, smoking chimney that spews sparks into the darkening evening sky. The hard earth that gets springy and elastic for a few metres as if threatening to swallow you. Later, they tell me that Auschwitz was built on an extensive swamp, and the springy places are above the underground draining ditches that are still full of water. But there is no time for looking around. The big, pyjama-clad henchmen of the Germans drive us along, shouting and beating us with their rubber hoses. Most of us are still in shock from the exhausting long journey without water or food, filthy with our own dirt, having been separated only a few minutes before from everyone and everything dear to us. They take us...where to? Suddenly, one man breaks out of the unit and runs with desperate howling toward the fence. The capos do not try to stop him. Bluish sparks! Machine gun fire!! The smell of burning flesh!!! There is no stopping, and anyone who turns around gets beaten.

There is a big dressing room with benches and numbered clothes racks above them. Hang up everything, shoes under the bench, remember the number. We are herded into another room. Behind a bench stand some ten or more barbers. First, shaving. I am sixteen years old and don't need it very much, but nobody asks me. They wipe the soap off with a towel that has seen better days. Forward, to the barbers at another bench. They shear off all the remaining hair, from the whole body, with a machine. Before

THE TUMBLER

the next room a capo hands us a bit of soap with RJF written on it. (Later they tell me that it stands for 'Rein Jüdisches Fett' - made from Jewish fat, but let's not go into that.) Where is the towel? There is no towel. We get into the shower room. Unbelievable. There is warm water. Heaven. The men begin to smile, enjoying the warm water. I have learned something and wash off the soap before the cold water, but I enjoy that too. I open my mouth, at last some drinking water. Everybody out. Into a third room. Where is the towel? There is no towel. We are wet and it is getting cold. Luckily, it is May and not December.

We wait, and at last they bring in two pushcarts, one with clothes and another one with shoes. Everyone gets a pair of long, thin underpants, pants, a shirt, a coat and a cap, all of which is of the same blue and white stripped pyjama-like fabric. At last, either Dutch wooden clogs or leather shoes, with a wooden sole. The capo says something in Slovak to a man before me; the man speaks only Hungarian and does not understand him. I volunteer to translate it for the capo and, at the same time, explain to him that I would like to get my own shoes back, because I have flat feet. He looks me intently up and down, points to the hose in his hand and says in German: 'Das ist mein Dolmetcher' (that is my translator) and whacks the poor man on his back: he understands at once. He gives me a pair of size 43 shoes (I wear five sizes smaller), gives me a no less hearty slap in the face - I understand too - and a pair of foot-cloths, (which you wear instead of socks). There is no end to miracles. Outside I find a half-open straw-mattress, stuff my shoes half full with straw, put on the foot-cloth and I am set.

The capo lines us up in threes and explains that when we meet a German, on the command 'Mützen ab!' we doff our caps. Nobody asks for a translation. We arrive at our block: it is like the other ones, some fifty metres long and twelve metres wide. Along the long walls, on both sides, two and half metre wide plank-beds in three storeys, one above the other; on every plank-bed, that are devoid of any mattresses or suchlike luxuries, there are five coarse blankets. In the middle of the block there runs a one-metre high and two-metre wide wall, for the capos' helpers. In the door stands *my* capo with the *translator* in his hand, shouting to get in faster. He recognises me and tells me to stand by the side. In the meantime two of his helpers shout and beat the people and drive them up on the planks, five on every one while I wait and tremble from fear, but try not to show it.

In the meantime I see that my capo is not a capo, but a 'Blockälteste', a block-commandant, which means that he is next in rank to God.

This gentleman takes me by the hand and leads me to his private room, just after the door. In the room there is a bed, a cupboard, a table, and a chair. On the table lies a whole loaf of bread. He looks at me, waiting for my reaction to this pomp and luxury, but I am new and am unable to appreciate properly what I see. He sets me on the bed, and says to me, 'Today you got the first, but by no means the last, slap in the face, and you got that one to help you to remember the following rules that could help you remain alive, perhaps, for some time: don't be between the first and or the last ones; don't be in the first row if you can avoid it; don't speak to a capo, or worse still, to a German if he does not speak to you first, and above all, never, never look them in the eyes.'

After this speech, he thinks a bit, gives me a quarter of the bread and waits, so it seems, for me to fall before his feet with tears of gratitude. If it had happened two months later I really would have done but, as I said, I was new, fat and not very hungry. So I just said 'thank you' nicely, and thought to myself that it seems that even between these hangman's helpers there are some with human feelings. The next day I saw him beat a boy half dead because he had stepped out of the line. But his advice I remembered, and that was partly why I survived. The advice and blind luck.

Five o'clock in the morning. Shouting, beatings; everybody out! The latrine is a bench of concrete, with holes in it. How can you do it like that? It seems that you can. What do you do? Better, don't ask. There are some water-taps. Most wash only their hands and eyes, but I take off the shirt. The water is cold, but refreshing. On the other hand, it is refreshing, but very cold. The next day, I too wash only my eyes, and there are many who don't do even that.

At half past six, they bring the 'coffee' with a piece of bread. I remember the bread from yesterday and give some to a friend, without explanation. I eat the rest of my bread, making sure they do not see it. Interesting, how much better it tasted than yesterday, and in two more weeks it will be a delicacy.

Seven o'clock, 'Zählappel' - counting. We are standing five abreast. Counting once, counting twice. Somebody leaves the row having something urgent to tell a friend. After the beating with the hose and the slaps in the face, hopefully he won't do it tomorrow. Counting, the third time. In our block everything is OK. In the other block there is one man less. The SS does not come until everything tallies. At last they find the missing one. He hid himself in the block under the blankets. Three capos beat him as a warning example. They count again, everything tallies. One capo goes to tell the SS and with the other capo we practice the 'Mützen ab!' command.

Then a German sergeant comes and counts the rows again. Incredible, everything tallies. Dismiss! It is only ten o'clock but everybody is waiting for the midday meal. Suddenly, shouting, howling, let's do the whole thing again. Fall-in! Open the rows! Take off your clothes! Yes, the underpants too. Put them before your feet. What happened? We add a new word to our vocabulary: selection. The capos are very nervous too; they run around between the rows, tell everybody to do their best to look healthy, strong and young, but not too young. A cloud covers the sun, and it begins to rain. We are naked. The clothes get wet. What do we do? We do nothing. If somebody tries to move, three capos fall over him. They are afraid too. From ear to ear, they whisper that the 'Angel of Death', Dr Mengele, (Dr Josef Mengele – a ruthless Nazi concentration camp doctor) is coming to make sure there were no damaged goods left after yesterday's selection.

Azriel Feuerstein

It is evident that such a personality won't leave his office in the rain: his boots could get dirty, God forbid! Luckily, the rain stops after half an hour. We do exercises, to get a bit warmer. I, too, understand that it won't do to stand inspection with chattering teeth, and try to run on the spot. The great man is here. It is possible that for many people the pope is God's representative on the earth, but here in Auschwitz, Dr Mengele is the undisputed master of life and death. White gloves, black uniform, gleaming black boots. On my right, a lean, young boy. He takes him out. The doctor stands before me. I learned something from the advice of my capo yesterday, and look straight at his chin, not higher. The man on my left is taken out too. A pack of capos surround them and take them to the gate, naked as they are. We may put on our clothes. I see that the coat of the man on my left, who won't need it any more, seems warmer and change it quickly. Where do they take those who were selected? There are some who say they were taken for lighter work. Yes, even here in Auschwitz. But nobody wants to change places with them.

According to the position of the sun and the stomach rumbles, it must be after midday. Where is the food? The vats arrive and with them a gangling boy with the tin soup-plates. There are not enough plates for all, so two people share one plate of soup. Some weeks later, when the hunger becomes *hunger*, this would be the cause of bloody fights. But it is only our second day on the planet Auschwitz and we are only just beginning to become animals, so there are not many fights.

My capo stands by the vat, and when he sees me he puts onto my plate a full portion from the bottom of the vat, where the soup is the thickest. Again, such a thing after two more weeks would be the cause of deep happiness and be a subject to talk about for a long time, but we are new. It is true that I am hungry, but the soup tastes terrible and after three mouthfuls - there are no spoons – I give the rest to my friend from home, Erdelyi Feri, who tells me to eat more if I want to survive. I try, but am unable to take more. Feri has no such problems. I see that the boy who brought the plates goes to sit down behind the block.

THE TUMBLER

The whole day I looked over the fences in every direction to see where the older people and children are, but could not see them. (You have to understand that Auschwitz was a complex consisting of many camps, each one surrounded by barbed wire fences and their own watchtowers and gates.) I thought they must be in some camp farther away. I went after the boy because, looking at his clothes and the number sewn above his pocket, I saw that he must be a long-termer. I spoke to him in German and Slovak, which is close to Polish. He told me that he is two years older than me, from the ghetto of Lemberg and has been in Auschwitz for a year. I asked him, 'Please, where are our parents?' He looked at me, and made a smoke-like gesture in the air and said, indifferently, 'Crematorium.'

Being a man with a short fuse, I got very angry at this spreader of rumours, and simply threw him. Luckily, we were behind the block so nobody saw us. After the war, when everybody knew what had happened to the old and the children, I thought to myself what an idiot I was that, even there, in the shadow of the crematorium's chimney, I was unable to look and see the terrible facts before my eyes. Later I forgave myself, and saw that I was not an idiot, but that the world around me had gone mad.

After the meal we got some time off and heard from the people with the vats that they would soon take us to work, where you have to take big stones from one place to another and back under the loving supervision of the SS and the capos with their hoses, but it seems that not yet. Now they take us to register and get our number. After two hours, they get to me. Name, father's name, mother's name, address? Everybody gets a round piece of coarse linen, with a number printed on it, hanging on a string. My name from now on is 37278 and tomorrow they will tattoo it on my arm. If you lose the number…the rest you already know.

After the registration they take us to a third camp and we have to stand before a wall that is full of bullet holes. They say that it is called the wall of death. Before the wall there is a bench. They will hang the man who tried to escape, but before that his capo gets beaten. Two capos beat him with hoses. In the beginning he shouts, but his howling ceases long before the end of the beating. The hanging I don't see: I close my eyes.

They take us back to *our* camp. What do we talk about after the horror that we witnessed? About the evening meal we are going to get, of course. The vats arrive. This time we are divided into two groups, as per the number of plates. We get a bowl of coffee, a piece of bread and a spoonful of marmalade. You have to hurry because the second group waits impatiently for the plates. It is unbelievable how much better the bread tastes after only one day.

We talk with the vat bearers. They are Polish. Their war began four years ago. Their story is a known one, but for us, still new. When the Germans occupied Poland, most of the Jews of the small villages were killed within a few weeks. The luckier ones were concentrated in ghettos in bigger cities. From there most of them were taken from time to time to extermination camps, and the rest were deported to concentrations camps. Here, few survived the selections, and most of those who did worked in the kitchen. We see that above the pocket of their jacket there is their number and, by its side, a yellow triangle that identifies them as Jews. Green triangles are for the criminals; they are mostly long termer Germans, usually capos. Red triangles are for the political prisoners, and if they are Jews too – many are – on the red triangle there is a yellow one, forming the Star of David. We learn that Auschwitz was built by Slovak Jews, of whom very few survived. All that does not help us much. About the high chimney spewing smoke and sparks, and about the strange smell in the air, for some reason nobody asks. Howling, shouting, beatings: curfew. We sleep. Our second night in Auschwitz.

The next day is a sunny, spring day, 19 May 1944. We got only the black, lukewarm water they call here 'coffee', without bread. Again, counting, and again it takes two hours. They say that they are taking us to work, but no. The capo comes and tells us to go and wash and prepare ourselves for selection, but this time for something good, or so he says. We open the rows; there is no need to strip. There comes a Wehrmacht officer, who is not in the SS, and it seems that the whole thing is not pleasant for him as he looks uncomfortable. You see that he is trying to take everyone. He asks if somebody wants to remain in Auschwitz; incredibly, some ten men choose to remain. It seems that they have found some friends who work in the kitchen and promised to help them. They return to the block.

When the officer hears that we had no breakfast, he takes us to the kitchen and everybody gets a piece of bread and coffee. That is not the end of the miracles: he takes us to exchange our rags. Is it possible that we got them only yesterday? We are given nearly new ones, and they even try to make them more or less fit. We only have to hold the numbers and keep them because the tattooists are not here, so there'll be no tattoos on our arms. They finish with changing our shoes too: the new ones also have wooden soles, but they are closer to the size I wear. As I did not give back my foot-clothes, I now have two pairs, so I am more comfortable. Now, in our new pyjamas we look almost human. We register for transport by our numbers.

The next day after breakfast, the wagons are already waiting. They are closed wagons, but we are only forty people in each one with an armed soldier sitting in the middle, so everybody has enough space to sit. There are some who think that perhaps they are taking us to be shot, but not I. I trust the Germans: they are frugal people and won't give us new clothes and waste a quarter of bread which they gave us for the journey only to shoot us. After ten hours we arrive.

Los, los! We have arrived straight into hell. An SS officer, as if cut out straight from some horror-movie, square, red faced, rimless eyeglasses, with a handgun in his right hand and a lash in his left one, runs around howling and beating everybody unlucky enough to be near him. Near the rails there are parts of new blocks which he wants us to take to the camp that is some hundreds of metres away, and do it 'SCHNELL! SCHNELL!' (quickly).

He wants two people to take a part, which would not be easy even for four. He rants and raves and shoots between the feet of the men and prances in rage. He does not mind the work: on the contrary, like the sadist he is, he enjoys the beating and frightening of the men. People fall down under the weight and he lashes their faces, smiling. A sturdy man, whose countenance commands respect somehow even in these pyjamas, goes to help a boy rolling about in pain. The Nazi lifts his lash but does not complete the movement. Another man, whom I can't describe in any other way than having the face of a murderer, goes and lifts the other side of the block-part taking it out of the beaten boy's hands. I take its third corner and decide then and there that those two people I won't let out of my eyes.

Later, I hear that the man who went to help the boy is Dr Fischbein, who commands respect everywhere, whatever the circumstances. He is around thirty-five years old and an advocate from Ungvar, with whom I'll talk a lot in the next weeks. The other one, with the face of a murderer, is Fischer, with whom I do not exchange a word other than 'good morning' but whom I follow as a shadow. I have no cause to regret my choice as this face of a murderer is never beaten or shouted at, not by the capos, and not even by the SS. I am convinced that this spur of a moment decision, to remain as close as possible to these two men, helped me to survive.

We arrive at the gate of KZ Wolgsberg. Later, they tell me that it is a concentration camp for work, and not for extermination. The difference between the two kinds of camps is that, in the first one, work is the main purpose, and death is only a by-product of overwork and starvation. In the second one, work is the by-product. My impression was that this animal who welcomed us would do everything to turn this camp into the latter. In the meantime, all the block-parts have been taken to the camp without a single death. I understand that there is an order against killing people for fun, otherwise I'm sure this monster would have killed at least a few.

This camp was a branch camp of KZ Gross-Rosen near the village of Hausdorf. It was built in a gently sloping clearing in the forest. At the end of the slope were the public buildings and the Appelplatz where the counting was held every morning and evening. On the slope there were round rooms, like Mongol yurts, for the inmates. Every such round room was six metres in diameter with a door on the southern side and a round hole in the ceiling for ventilation and light and, some ten-centimetres above it, a slightly larger cover against the rain. There was a wooden bench to sit on and to hold the loose straw on which we slept. The 'wall' of this construction was no more than half a centimetre thick and looked like cardboard. Surprisingly, the whole thing was much more comfortable than it sounds: it was not too hot on summer days and not too cold on chilly nights, had good ventilation, and was not even too dark. On the slope there were five rows of such yurts, six in every row, and twenty men in each room. This description should be taken with a pinch of salt, as some of my memories that I wrote about at this particular time are somewhat faded now and it may be that some details are wrong.

Before the meal everybody got a mess tin and a spoon. The same officer who brought us from Auschwitz stood by the vats, supervising and saw to it that we got soap for washing the dishes. He announced that after the meal everybody would get another blanket. The soup would not have been bad if that SS animal did not run about shouting and lashing everyone in sight. We got a quarter of bread with a piece of salami, got our blanket and went to our room. We slept in twos, putting one blanket under us on the straw and using two more for cover. Before going to sleep I went out and found Fischer sharpening the handle of the spoon into a knife on a stone. He then cut two slices of bread for the following day, put them into the mess tin together with the spoon, then into a carton that he bound around him with a string. I went down to the kitchen and found some cartons and string. I took some for the doctor too. I did everything that Fischer had done, returned to the room and was justly celebrated for the inventions.

It was still dark when the wake-up alarm, accompanied by the usual shouting and beating, was sounded. We got coffee and I ate my bread from the day before. Then came the familiar counting and after that we were divided into 'Kommandos', or work places. I got into 'Baukommando Dübcner'. Now we were counted again, this time by work places. I was sure that it was not the end. The SS officer with the lash came to supervise the counting. He beat the capos because the counting took too long, but I knew that he had something else up his sleeve.

There was a small group of people whose language nobody could understand. They were Jewish prisoners of war from the Greek army who built the camp under the loving care of this animal, as could be seen from their lash-marred faces that were only skin and bones and from their terrified eyes. This pride of the German Army told two capos to bring a sturdy bench and, with immense satisfaction, made a speech: 'Here is a man who stole bread from the kitchen and is even more guilty because he was the leader of this group. Now he will get his just punishment.'

They then brought a tall and fearfully thin man, stripped to the waist, whose every bone could be seen under the skin and whose bones were full of bumps from previous beatings. The capos bound him to the bench and the two capos commenced to beat him, one with a stick and the other with a hose. This criminal sadist, who called himself an officer, counted with a satisfied smile the number of lashes, and when everybody saw that after ten the poor boy was mercifully dead, the capos had to finish the full twenty-five. This was the first – but not the last - dead man I was to see in my life.

We went to work feeling very depressed. It was clear to everyone that, in the hands of this beast, it wouldn't take long before we would all look no better than that poor boy. When we went out of the camp, the officer who took us out from Auschwitz was standing by the gate and took the doctor with him.

We walked some three kilometres and came to a field where we had to dig a trench for a railroad. Everybody got a shovel and a pickaxe, and we were dispersed along the line. I, of course, went after Fischer. Behind the line, every fifty metres or so, stood an armed soldier and if somebody wanted to go behind the bushes, he had to ask him for permission. These soldiers did not bother about the work as usual, but there were some who got bored without shouting. The foremen, or 'Meisters', were Poles of German origin, who explained and controlled the work and, except for some shouting and cursing, did not do much harm. That was the job of the capos but even they began to beat and bellow only when some SS came to supervise. We had to dig a not too deep trench, some three metres wide at the bottom and five metres wide at the level of the terrain.

The first thirty centimetres were not too difficult as that was the black mother earth or the 'Mutterboden', but under that the earth got yellow, hard and full of stones and you had to use the pickaxe a lot. The foreman's chief concern was to keep the two kinds of earth separate because they wanted to take the black earth away to use as topsoil on the gardens of the Germans. As work progressed, this digging got more and more difficult because the deeper you got, the farther you had to throw the earth. Fischer showed his mettle. He went to the foreman and suggested that two men take a stretch, separate the black earth and pile it up in small heaps outside the working area, so it would be easier to take it away. Fischer's face of a murderer helped to convince the Meister so he went to return the pickaxe, and I after him. I am not sure that, if Fischer had to choose his partner, I would have been the one as I produced more or less a half of what he did, but he did not say anything and neither did the foreman. The work was easier than digging with the pickaxe, but we were before the eyes of the capos and the soldiers who made sure that we did not rest for a moment. I pushed myself: they did not have to urge me because I did not want Fischer to fire me.

At twelve o'clock we had half an hour's rest and some coloured water that they called soup, but at least it was warm. We had eaten breakfast at five o'clock in the morning and this soup made us even hungrier. The work went on till four or five o'clock in the afternoon. The first two kilometres homeward were more difficult than in the morning, but the third one was worse. The problem was that the shoes with the wooden soles made my feet ache and I was not the only one. I saw that those boys, who came from poor homes and were used to walking bare-footed, put their shoes on their shoulders. We got to the gate of the camp. I was very glad to see that the Wehrmacht officer handled the counting because he did it fast and then sent us to eat. In the soup there were bits of noodles and unpeeled potatoes and I was surprised at the excellent taste of potato peels. We got a third of bread too and twenty grams of margarine. Then we went to the rooms, where I was very glad to see Dr Fischbein waiting for us. He told us that the officer, whose name was Captain Novak, would be the new commander of the camp instead of that SS beast.

Captain Novak wanted to make him a capo but Dr Fischbein declined, saying that he did not want to punish his fellow sufferers. Then the captain wanted him to work in the office, but after the doctor heard that the captain had asked to be commandeered to a unit that had no connection with camps, he did not accept this offer either. I was angry with him for not agreeing to work in the office, where he had a better chance of survival and perhaps even help his friends; but the doctor explained that if the captain were commandeered away, who knew what sadist would take his place?

The work on the railway bed took until July and Captain Novak remained in the camp until nearly the end of the job. My impression was that he tried to make it more bearable for us. He opened a small hospital where a doctor from my hometown worked, whose family name I have forgotten in spite of the fact that later he helped me a lot.

The Greek prisoners of war, of whom one died nearly every day, he assigned to clean the latrines where once a month they had to clean the pits but got double portion of everything, although for many of them it was too late.

At least once a week everyone had to go to the barbers who were responsible for the haircuts too. We were supposed to get a day off every second Sunday only, but on working Sundays he stopped work at midday and we went to bathe and change clothes. He made sure that the capos did not steal too much from the one thousand and six hundred calories we then still had to get for fourteen hours of hard work. Having said that, it has to be understood that the whole system was built so that, after some time, it would draw out the last drops of life force from everyone under its sway, and the efforts of one man could not reverse this process, only perhaps slow it down a bit. Novak was not part of those units whose duty it was to serve in camps, but was commandeered here after he was wounded on the front and he got the choice to transfer to the SS. That offer in itself shows that he was known as a true Nazi. Now, with us, he was halfway human due to the fact that his stomach was too weak for the job, or perhaps the approaching end of the war and the smell of German defeat in the air had a beneficial influence on his conscience.

After two days of suffering from aching feet, as a result of coming and going to work, I got rid of my wooden soled shoes, as others did. I mean that I threw them over my shoulder and tried to walk without them. At home I had walked only in orthopaedic shoes, and today, finalising this writing, I shudder even at the thought of walking barefoot. But, after I tried, it was easier than I had feared, and I wore my shoes only for working. It was around that time that I confessed to myself that I was suffering from hunger, like everyone else.

As I mentioned before, I came to Auschwitz as a fat boy, and for that reason I was ashamed to talk about hunger because I was afraid they would laugh at me and say that food was the only thing I thought about. This psychology and the fat on my body helped me for a while to conceal the hunger, even from myself. After some weeks, when the stealing of bread from each other got to be a daily event and you could not put down your bread without it being stolen, I too understood why hunger was the only thing you could think about. At meals you looked pop-eyed at the cook, at how deep he sank the ladle into the vat, because, if he was lazy and ladled from the top, you got the thin part of the soup without the potatoes or whatever. That remained the most interesting subject and was a question of life and death. It was even more important when we had milk soup with noodles, which happened once in a fortnight. Of course, the milk was mixed with water at the ratio of the mixed goose and horsemeat salami: one goose to one horse. Nevertheless, when, on the way home from work, we smelt the soup, we hastened our steps until we would be nearly running. Even now, writing this, I recall the smell and the taste in my mouth.

It was very important to place yourself correctly. On the one hand, you are very, very hungry and would like to be among the first ones. On the other hand, it stands to reason that there will be more noodles at the bottom of the vat and, therefore, you should try to be among the last ones. However, you should also know which cook stands by the vat. If, for example, it is Lolek then it is well known that he is very conscientious and sinks in the ladle all the way every time, and with him it is possible that, contrary to all expectations, the soup at the bottom will be thinner. Everybody had his theory, which was a result of deep thoughts and painful self-doubt. I did not talk about my theory, which was very simple: I did my best to stand in line either after the doctor or after Fischer (the ideal way would be, of course, to stand between the two, but that seldom happened). Both of them, without fail, got served from the bottom of the kettle: Dr Fischbein out of respect, and Fischer because they were afraid of him. The one behind them got part of the bounty, but if you could not get the two of them, Fischer was the better bet. In the beginning these considerations were discussed in a sarcastic vein, but soon, when the hunger became *hunger*, they became very earnest indeed. Hunger was not the only subject yet, but it remained in the background all the time.

The food did not contain the necessary vitamins, and therefore the wounds healed very slowly. The teeth got weaker and there were deaths now, not only among the Greeks, but also among us, the newcomers. They had to make a special place in front of the office for the men who died that day, and these dead men had to be taken into account in the daily counting. Once every few days a truck from Gross-Rosen came to take away the dead for cremation there. Those who were taken away had to be taken off the number of prisoners who had to be accounted for. That was the job of the office worker, the 'Schreiber', who one day failed to do it, and at the next day counting, one person was missing. We had to stand for five hours in the Appelplatz and could not go to work until a soldier on a motorcycle got back from Gross-Rosen with a letter saying that a dead man from our camp was delivered there for cremation. That was the first and only time I saw Captain Novak strike somebody, and I must say, that he did it with all his heart so that the Schreiber's face was swollen for a whole week. That day we worked till darkness and remembered the Schreiber, his mother and other relatives often and harshly.

The work on the railway was nearly finished and the work with the black earth got harder as we had to take it with wheelbarrows to the trucks and load it. Still it was better than lugging around the heavy rails and sleepers. The work got harder and more dangerous with the arrival of a young SS officer who was of Schwabish origin and spoke Hungarian. He had a big wolfhound with him and they bellowed together. He was always shouting at the capos because they didn't beat the people who stopped for a moment to wipe off their sweat.

Two weeks before the end of work on the railway, on a Sunday morning, there was a parade after the counting to honour the new camp commandant, a sergeant major of the skull-and-bones unit of the SS, the official guards of the concentration camps. We were very much afraid of these changes, but the first days passed without the situation getting worse, and in some ways it even got better. Every room in turn was called after work to the shoemaker's shop where they exchanged the wooden-soled shoes for leather soled ones, and the sergeant was there to see that each one got his size. In each sole there were a certain number of nails and we got an order to go to the shoemaker every time a nail got lost. That was the commandant's hobbyhorse and at the morning musters he inspected the shoes. If someone did not have the necessary number of nails, he got slapped in the face with enthusiasm. Therefore, we named the commandant 'the Schuster'. My new shoes were much more comfortable than the previous ones, but I still only wore them at work as I had become used to coming and going without them.

Azriel Feuerstein

His other hobbyhorse was cleanliness, and that is why I am nearly deaf to this very day. It happened some days after the work at the railway was finished. The new project was the urgent building of a number of two-storey houses for the Germans fleeing before the Russian Army. The cause of the urgency and the purpose of the houses we learned from the Polish foremen, through the doctor who spoke their language. Anyway, on an especially hot day, when we came home exhausted from the day's work, I saw from the corner of my eye that somebody, who had to relieve himself urgently, had left his mark near the wall of our room and, like the rest, did my best not to notice it. After only some minutes there came a shout: 'Room 20/3 (that was our room), out!' and with that two capos were already inside beating everyone.

Outside, the sergeant major, red in the face, was already there to personally take part in the proceedings. It seems that in the course of his daily inspection he had seen the not so fragrant offering near the wall. Not only that but the room itself looked, in his words, like a pigsty: two blankets were not rolled up and there were some bits of straw in the middle. We had to stand in a row in front of the room, and it turned out that I was the second in spite of what I had learned in Auschwitz, which was to always be in the middle. The sergeant major continued his speech saying that he would teach us, 'Saujuden', Jewish swine that we were in a civilised country and not in the jungle. Everybody gets beaten. The capo with the rubber hose brought a chair and laid the first man on it.

I don't know how many strokes he got as I was too occupied with my thoughts to count, but they told me, twenty. After they had finished with the first one, and laid him down because he was unable to stand, and before they laid me, who was second, on the chair, I said in German, 'Sir, you are not right, it is not our fault because we were out working the whole day.' He got even redder and bellowed straight into my face, 'What did you say, du Saujude, I have no right?!' With that he tore away the hose from the capo's hand and hit me with it over the head with such a force

121

that one end of the hose hit one ear and the other end with his fist hit my other ear. I was dazzled for a few minutes and my left ear bled, but I did not faint. I reflected on the fact that the whole thing happened because of a linguistic misunderstanding: I meant to say in German that he is unjust, and not that he had *no* right.

They did not continue the beating and the others were very thankful, especially Dr Fischbein, who stood after me. The sergeant major went down the slope, fuming under his Hitler moustache, 'I have no right? I have no right? You dirty Jews, I will show you what rights I have!' I was sure that after all that he would take his rage out on me every time, but that did not happen for some reason. Perhaps he did not remember faces.

12

'Fugenmeister'

The next day neither the one who got the full twenty strokes, nor I, went to work: we stayed in the sickroom. The doctor said that I did not have a concussion, but I was still a bit dizzy, and I did not hear at all in my left ear. It got better after a few days, but ever since then my hearing in both my ears has become slowly, but steadily worse.

The boy who got the twenty strokes did not get better, and later I heard that they took him back to Auschwitz. The doctor from my hometown Kassa, whose name was Jozsi, told me that he knew my father and that if the work got too much, he would get me a few days in the hospital. He did not have to explain to me how risky it was there, as we both knew that a visit from a German 'medical delegation' that came to inspect from time to time was more dangerous than any kind of sickness. He gave me some vitamin tablets too and asked me not to tell anyone. These tablets were black, huge and tasted terrible. We once got one with a meal, but most of us threw it away because we did not believe the Germans. Dr Jozsi said that they did help and they would make the wound on my ankle heal faster. I asked him to send me back to work because I knew that the Lager Commandant, the 'Schuster', came to visit the sickroom from time to time and I thought it healthier if we didn't meet.

We began the new building project in good spirits. The fact that the buildings were for German refugees, who were fleeing before the Russian Army, gave us new hope. After a week or so we got the news that on 6 June 1944 the Western Powers had landed in France and opened the long awaited second front. It seemed that the end of the war was very near. Dr Fischbein was sure that he would soon meet his beloved wife and three year old daughter and we would all meet our parents and relatives. The doctor was on furlough from the Hungarian Labour Service at the time of the deportation from his hometown, Ungvar, and instead of returning, he chose to go to Auschwitz with his family. We asked neither him nor ourselves if we really believed that we would meet our loved ones again.

While talking about the end of the war, we all believed, or tried to believe, that everything would be as it had before. I, myself, when I went to sit down on our free Sundays in a desolated corner of the camp near the spring to recall the moments at home, did not think about my parents as dead, and was only sorry that I was unable to think about them for longer. Thoughts about the meals and cakes interfered and took up most of my time. Now, writing these words, I have no other explanation why, in spite of all we had seen and lived through, we were still more or less normal in a world that had gone completely insane.

We could feel that the building project was very urgent as high-ranking SS officers inspected the site nearly every day, and they hurried the soldiers, who hurried the foremen, who shouted at the capos, who beat us. That perhaps made us work somewhat faster but there was an increase in accidents and more dead, and work was so important that if someone was unable to work because of the beating, the capo got chewed out.

At the beginning, the field had to be levelled and for that we had to transport the earth from place to place in narrow-tracked trucks. I was unable to find Fischer, my good-luck charm, and promptly got my hand crushed between a rock and a rail. It hurt terribly but I went to the hospital only in the evening, after the meal of course. Dr Jozsi put a salve on it and bandaged it up, but one of my fingers has remained crooked to this very day. The next day I took good care not to let Fischer out of my sight. He saw that they brought a new concrete mixer and went straight to the head foreman and said that he had much experience with this kind of machine, and wonder of wonders, it was true. I brought sand to the mixture, and it was not a bad occupation, and no capo came near us.

The foundation plates for fifteen houses were poured first and after that came the carpentry work which the foremen did themselves. In these plates, all around, there were holes ninety centimetres from each other for the pillars that held up the roof and the construction of the walls. The pillars were built from bricks that were thirty centimetres wide and twenty-five centimetres high and deep with holes for building irons and concrete. On both sides of the bricks there were two V-shaped gaps that served as rails for the bricks of the wall. These bricks themselves were ninety centimetres wide, the same height as that of the bricks of the pillars and some six centimetres thick with holes for isolation. The bricks were put in the rail-like gaps of the pillars on both the inside and the outside of the wall and the initial plan was to fill the gap between them with earth. However, it was later decided that there was not enough time for that, and that the air between them was sufficient isolation. The bricks were held together by mortar.

When the wall reached a two and a half metre height, we poured concrete in the holes of the pillar with the irons, and we poured the concrete for the ceiling that was the foundation for the second storey. All this procedure was shorter than this explanation and looked not bad at all. The walls inside the house were built on the same principle, but with one brick only. The bricks of the walls were not plastered, and, being uncoated, the line of mortar between the bricks had to be straitened and the bricks themselves had to be clean. These lines were called 'fugen'. Here, I took the initiative: I found a new, two-centimetre wide mortar spoon and guessed that its purpose was to smooth the mortar between the bricks. I saw that Fischer, who in the meantime had been promoted to bricklayer (with me as his helper of course), had enough bricks at hand. I took the mortar spoon, a bucket of water and some rags and began to smooth the fugen and clean the bricks. For once, I was in luck: the chief engineer together with the chief foreman went by, when I finished a wall.

THE TUMBLER

They liked my work very much so Fischer got another helper and I got promoted to 'Fugenmeister'.

It seemed to be light work, but it was not exactly so. The first rows of bricks were no problem. But even here you had to hurry and finish the cleaning before the mortar dried. It was not as easy with the higher rows. True, Fischer built scaffolding that I could use for the inside, but for the outside I had to help myself. I found two pulleys, some ropes and a plank, which I anchored on the building irons on top of the pillars and I was in business. I sprang like a monkey from one side of the wall to the other with my machine and did not need Fischer's scaffolding. I was very proud of my invention: I was self employed, they seldom disturbed me and, whenever there was an inspection of higher-ups, the chief foreman, who promoted me, showed off with the finish of the walls and his 'Fugenmeister'.

Time passed. It was already the end of August and the winds got chillier in the evenings as autumn approached. The first storeys of the houses were nearly finished and the next day they had to pour the concrete for the ceiling of the first storey and basis for the second one. Everybody took part in this work that began earlier than usual and you didn't go home until the pouring was finished. The wounds on my ankles were in bad shape so I decided to go to the hospital and ask Dr Jozsi for a few days off. He cleaned the wounds and gave me two days to rest. The next day, after the usual morning visit, he came running back, called me outside and gave me a slip sending me back to work while hurriedly explaining that there was an SS 'medical inspection' coming and I'd better get out the back way. Later, they told me that it was a selection and that they sought the young, the weak and those who were in hospital for more than two weeks, for sending them back to Auschwitz: a hundred and fifty in all. However, on my way out I met an SS officer coming out of the bathroom and he sent me out to the waiting selected group. I tried to explain that I was sent back to work and that I was the Fugenmeister, but to no avail. I tried to slip away, but another SS officer sent me back. I saw that they began to write down the numbers and at the last moment, when the capo turned away for a minute, I somehow ran away. I was very glad that I did and was proud of my courage, but let's us not forget that after that there remained in the group a hundred and fifty men, less one. They simply took somebody else in my place.

The next day. I am sitting on my unsteady plank on the second storey on the side of the building, some twenty metres above the road. I am doing my work, whistling, glad of my escape. Suddenly, on the road under me, I hear shouting, weeping, and the screaming of 'Shema Yisroel' approaching. I look down and there, on the road under me, I see an open truck with the hundred and fifty people one on top of each other, naked but for skimpy underpants in the chilly winds. I trembled from fear, got hold of the rope, the plank shook and the bucket of water fell down. I was lucky though, since at least it did not fall on the road. To go down there you had to get permission from the post that was the young Hungarian speaking SS officer with the wolfhound, whom it was always safer not to meet, and who had taken a special dislike of me for my privileged work. Up to that day I did not know what acrophobia, the fear of heights, was. This fear is with me to this very day and when I see someone on TV walking near a precipice, I am unable to look.

From that day on the situation got steadily worse. The cold winds of September, the murky skies, the leaden rain in small drops were not enough to stop the work, and we got frozen to the bones. The thin clothes got wet in the morning and did not dry out during the night, even though we slept in them. The wounds on my ankles got worse day by day and my work, which up to now I had always begun in good spirits and which enabled me to forget even the hunger, was now a long day of suffering, pain and fear. It did not help that from then on we only got a quarter of bread, instead of the usual third, but the worst was this newly acquired fear of high places. As long as the work was inside, I did not mind it so much even on the scaffolding, but outside on that plank which hung unsteadily in the wind, it began to be unbearable. I held the rope with desperation, trembling from head to toe, and sweat in spite of the cold. It was clear that I had to do something, if I wanted to survive. I hesitated in going anywhere near the hospital because of my last experience; yet I knew that either the fever from the infection of my wounds or the unsteady plank that made me crazy would bring me to the sickroom in a few days anyway, not on my own feet, but with broken limbs.

I was not the only one to be in a bad way. The cold wind was the forerunner of the nearing Schlezian winter. Every day there were more corpses before the office. The stomach-tearing hunger, and the fact that the good news we heard from the front did not seem to bring the end of the war any nearer for us, all contributed to the loss of hope. Dr Fischbein was the only one who tried to encourage us, but there were fewer people around him to hear it. The only one who did not change was Fischer. He too got thinner from hunger, but it seemed that it affected him less. Even his clothes seemed drier. I was convinced that, even if we all died, he would be the last one.

One day, while on the plank, I closed my eyes. The sound of the falling bucket woke me up at the last minute and I found myself holding the rope with a desperate effort, while half my body was hanging over the precipice. I decided then and there that I wouldn't climb on that plank any more and I went to the hospital. The hope that I would get a piece of bread from Dr Jozsi was part of that decision.

Later in the evening, when there were fewer people waiting outside, Dr Jozsi cut off the bandages on my ankle, smelt the stench of the pus, took my temperature and from the look on his face I saw that I was in a bad way. In spite of that, I seemed to be in luck because he told me that the day before he was in Wüstegiersdorf, in the central hospital for all the camps of Gross-Rosen, half an hour away, and that the chief surgeon there was a good friend of his. There were some medicines there that were not available here. He promised to give me a letter to him, but also told me that the commandant of this institution was an SS sergeant major, a dangerous animal, whom it was better to avoid. He said that actually I had no choice because if I stayed here, it would be the end of me within a short time. It turned out that this saved my life. The piece of bread that he gave me I appreciated even more, when you saw that he would very much have liked to eat it himself. I am proud of myself for not asking for it. The next day they took us to the hospital in Wüstegiersdorf.

13

Conversations about Faith

'Welcome, Fröken Ulle, how was the visit at home? I hope that everybody is well.'

'Yes, thank God, everybody is OK. It's always very nice to visit the folks. In the evenings I read your story and corrected some sentences, but I want to say, that if we take into account that you were not born here, there were very few mistakes to correct and that only in the structure of some sentences could one feel that you don't write in your native tongue, but that I did not want to touch.'

'Yes, I am lucky in that I have a retentive visual memory. But on the other hand, since I got that beating on my ears, I can't remember anything complicated by hearing only. Thank you, Fröken Ulle, for wasting your time correcting my writing. This is something I did not even dare to ask.'

'I really did it with pleasure, Yeory, but there is something I wanted to ask. At the end of the first part, you write that your mother's desperate cry in Auschwitz cut your life into two unequal parts. What did you mean by that?'

I took a breath before giving my long answer, 'Well, my life was simply cut into two unequal parts, as I wrote: up to that time I was the only and pampered son of a well-to-do family, safe in his surroundings and, like his peers and classmates, someone who could reasonably plan his future.

'From that cry in Auschwitz, my life had less worth than that of any beast of burden unprotected by any law. To kill it and torture it was not only permitted, but a laudable duty. The two parts are unequal in their quality, content and, I hope, length because the first part was sixteen years only and the second will hopefully be longer.

'The two parts are unequal also in that in the first, I was a loved member of a big, warm, closely knit family, who always had somebody to turn to, whereas now I am here alone, in a foreign land. I had a language that I loved, was well versed in its poetry, literature and used this knowledge with confidence, and now that language is totally useless to me.

'Even if I am capable of learning new languages comparatively easily, I will never be able to use them and know them as I knew Hungarian when I was sixteen years old, and not even Hungarian because I shall forget it. Very unequal even in personal safety and confidence because, after what happened, I know that it can happen, that they can take you one day and turn you into an animal. The fact that it happened shows that it can happen and there will always be forces to try it again. And as long as I live, I shall always ask myself if I should not have jumped off that platform in Auschwitz, gone with those who went to their death and shared their fate.

'Above all, I am more convinced than ever, even as I was before the Holocaust that we, Jews, should live in our own country like all other nations do. I am sorry, Fröken Ulle, that you got such a longwinded and depressing explanation that has so little in common with this, seldom seen, glorious weather outside.'

Fröken Ulle took an equally hard breath before replying, 'Forgive me for saying this, Yeory, but you have an annoying habit of always ending a serious conversation with a cynical remark, which can sometimes be irritating. I know that you won't like it, but now, when I was at home, I had a serious conversation about you with my pastor and spiritual leader who has helped me in difficult and sad situations. He said that belief in God and faith in Him is a great help in every difficult situation as well as a source of strength, and that you too should find a source of strength in the fact that from so many who did not, you were chosen to survive. He said that you should understand that the

Azriel Feuerstein

Almighty had plans for you, a purpose you can't see yet. It is difficult to bear and endure a bitter fate without that faith in a God who has not only the power, but the right too, to dispose of our fate, and whose decisions eventually benefit us, even if we are unable to see it so at that time. That is why we, Christians, pray everyday that His will be done in the same prayer that we pray for our daily bread.

'My pastor said that the fact that the Jewish people have suffered so much in the course of time shows that these people have a very important role in His plans and that the sufferings were sent to strengthen them for this role. He asked me to do everything in my power to persuade you to pray, or at least to say that prayer for the dead, the Kadish, if only for your parents who had faith.'

I replied, 'Even if it is difficult for me to believe that the Power that controls our lives is always benevolent and merciful, about your good heart, Fröken Ulle, I have no doubt at all. I have no thought that it is usually less difficult to accept and explain the misfortunes of others than your own. And speaking about the Jewish faith, approximately at the time of the Christian Easter we have Pesah, the holiday of the unleavened bread. What I wanted to say is that on Pesah Eve, which is called the 'Seder', we have a prayer, a song that we used to sing and which says that not only Pharaoh wanted to destroy us, but that in every generation there are those who want to destroy us, and God delivers us from their hands.

'Even as a child, I said to myself, how much easier it would be for Him, and chiefly for us, if instead of delivering us every time – those of us who were left – He wouldn't let us fall into their hands in the first place, and then He wouldn't have to disturb Himself and us in every generation.'

'Yeory,' answered Fröken Ulle, 'that cynical voice again! But come, let's drink our coffee before it gets cold and have some cookies too, because I have wanted to ask you something for a long time. You write that, in Auschwitz and in the later camps, you talked about seeing your family after the war, when it should

133

have been clear to you, after all you had seen, that they were no longer alive. How could that be? For you, of all people, who had seen the chimney in Auschwitz belching smoke, spark and smell, for you their death should have been evident, I think.'

I solemnly replied, 'I asked myself the same question. It is really very strange, but true. I spoke about this subject with many survivors and all said the same. What's more, people who stayed on in Auschwitz for many months in the shadow of that chimney and heard about the gas chambers tell the same tale of talking about how we would meet our families after the war... Why? I have no answer. But all that is true only for us, Hungarian Jews, who were comparatively new to this world. A few months are perhaps too short a time to comprehend the extent of the incomprehensible evil.'

Fröken Ulle probed further, 'I have another question that perhaps you won't like: if you, who were there, could not believe what you saw, why are you so sure that the Germans, who were not there and did not see what you did, lie in saying that they did not know?'

I replied, "I thought, Fröken Ulle, that you were driving at this. The sorry truth is that I have no answer. Let's say that the Germans of that era bear the original sin of this genocide forever, because, even if they did not exactly know the extent of the crimes committed in their names, they were silent partners in the murders, the robberies and the deportations. It should have been their duty to ask what was happening to the Jews and it should have been the duty of the Allied Forces too.

'We, Jews, have the right to hold the civilized world accountable and to condemn the Germans for being accomplices in the crimes or for being indifferent to them. It is very difficult for me to understand those many hundreds of thousands of Germans who took part in the Holocaust in various degrees. Let us begin with those lawyers and legal workers, who participated in the drafting of the discriminating laws, that made all that came after possible and legal; then those who gave the orders to enforce these laws and gave directions on how and where; those who organized, directed and executed the robbery of Jewish properties; those who ordered, directed and executed the concentration of Jews for deportation; those who drew up the timetable of the deporting trains most effectively and made those trains available in the first place in war-torn Germany; those who in the course of their daily work from nine to five disposed of the golden teeth that were torn out of the murdered before cremation; those who decided to what use to put the shorn off hair of the women and did it after eating their breakfast at home and then going to work.

'These people went home after work and, while caressing their loving daughters' blonde hair, thought about whether it is better to shave the hair of the murdered ones before or after the gas chamber. All these were ordinary people, not monsters, and they certainly did not see themselves as such. What makes me most afraid is the grey ordinariness of evil. Not the evil itself, but the ordinariness of it. But let's not speak of that, because this direction leads to madness. No, Fröken Ulle, let's not acquit the Germans from the charge of murder and of being accomplices to it before, during and after the fact.'

'I liked what you wrote about your work: that in those terrible circumstances of forced labour, filth and hunger, you had pride in your work and were glad when they prized you for it, that you, as "Fugenmeister", were able to make the walls beautiful and clean.'

'Yes, it seems stupid but even then there remained a kind of satisfaction in a job well done and in being, to a certain extent, independent in it, without being too much disturbed by the capos. Of course, the ubiquitous hunger was always in the background, but the feeling that you were able to solve the problems was important.'

'You were lucky to find this Dr Jozsi from your hometown,' said Fröken Ulle

'Yes, he helped me very much. Without his vitamin tablets the wounds on my ankles would have healed even more slowly. In retrospect I can say that I always had somebody or something that helped me back on my feet after a knockout of fate laid me on my back. That is one of the reasons why I call this book in your hands; "The Tumbler."'

'You helped yourself a lot too, as for example, when you were able to somehow escape from that group that was selected for Auschwitz.'

I replied, 'It goes without saying that I did whatever I could to save myself, but I didn't for a moment let myself forget that, instead of me, the Germans took someone else. They wanted a hundred and fifty people and they did not take less. My luck was perhaps somebody else's misfortune'

'OK, Yeory, it is getting dark and I have to go. See you tomorrow. I see that we have been talking too much and there are some cookies left. I'll leave them and hope that you'll find some use for them,' said Fröken Ulle with a twinkle in her eye.

'Don't worry, Fröken Ulle, I shall do my best for your sake, and the cookies too. Good night and goodbye,' I responded.

14

The Hospital and the Death March

Before we were loaded onto the open truck on our way to the hospital, they took all our clothes away and left only the thin underpants. It was around the end of October or beginning of November and although there was no snow yet, a kind of steady leaden rain and the cold wind made even our bones freeze. The logic of the Germans! They take us to the hospital to get well, but do their best to kill us on the way. We huddled together for warmth, but those who could not move were even worse off. A boy from Munkacs, who was in the hospital some weeks earlier, trembled not only from cold, but also from fear. He told us that the SS sergeant, named Horst, who was the commandant of the institution, threatened that if someone returned a second time, he wouldn't stay alive long. According to him, this Horst had a habit of welcoming the new patients with beatings and exercises to see if they were worth the expensive medicines - not that there were any expensive medicines there. The drive did not take more than half an hour, but it seemed much longer.

At last we got there, to the central hospital of the camps in Wüstegiersdorf. Because of the wounds on my ankles, I was among the last ones to get off the truck. A boy clad in the pyjama uniform of the prisoners, but with a white coat, helped me to descend. I looked at him, and did not believe my eyes. 'Johnny, is it you?!' I exclaimed. At first he did not recognise me and I had to explain to him that I am Gyuri Feuerstein, or what remains of him. It took him time to recover and he let me remain the last one. That Johnny, whom I was so glad to see, was an Austrian refugee Jew who had fled just in time in 1938, a few days after the

THE TUMBLER

German occupation of Austria, to Kassa where he found work in the haberdashery of Kürti, a relative of his and whose store was next to ours. Through his connections my father was able to get him permission to work and stay, and Johnny was very thankful and friendly with us. He too was an alarmist and 'spreader of rumours' who told everyone that we lived in a fool's heaven in Hungary and should seek ways to escape before it was too late. It seems that even he did not take his warnings to heart because he too was caught, as we were. Because he was a German speaker and educated, and because the officer who was the inspector of all the camp hospitals who visited here only once in a while was once his classmate, he got to be the 'Lagerschreiber', the office worker of the hospital and, as such, a dignitary there. Even Horst, the SS sergeant, was afraid of this inspector. All this, I got to know later, but at our first meeting he only warned me not to let on that we knew each other, put a vitamin tablet in my mouth and led me to my bed.

My first impression of the hospital was not too bad. The big room seemed airy and bright, with some thirty beds and bed sheets that were once white. The orderlies and doctors wore white coats, and the doctors had old-fashioned wooden stethoscopes in their pockets. It is true that there were two patients in every bed but you can't have everything. Johnny led me to the small room, where there were only five beds. It was not as bright as the big room but with less screams and quarrelling. He laid me down in a bed with an older man of only skin and bones and promised me that the man was going to die in a day or two, and he did.

In this room I stayed for at least one month with four and sometimes seven men – Johnny let me keep to my own bed – and I don't remember talking to anyone. The letter of Dr Jozsi, I gave to his friend, the chief doctor here. He put it in his pocket without saying anything, but if nobody was looking he pressed in my hand some vitamins or a better salve for my wounds. These wounds, named phlegmone, are caused by lack of vitamins. They ulcerate, are full of pus, reach the bones if they are not cured and are dangerous. Eight men died in the time I was there. There was one who had an appendix operation with only local anaesthesia and a razor blade because there was nothing else. The operation succeeded but the next day that animal, Sergeant Horst, heard that they were giving him medicine to ease his pains and ordered to stop it at once. The unfortunate man howled in pain the whole day, until Johnny and another orderly finished him off to end this situation. They had no other way, because if the doctor decided to give him some medicine in spite of the sergeant's orders, Horst would without doubt shoot the doctor there and then on the spot.

That is the only thing I remember about the hospital. I think that I must have been sleeping most of the time. My wounds got better, I did not have much pain and, thanks to Johnny, even the hunger was not so unbearable because when he brought the vat in at every meal, he let me be the last one, so I always got the thick part of the soup and a full portion. I was aware that this period in the hospital, and chiefly Johnny, saved my life for the time being, and *The Tumbler* was somehow on his feet again. But there is an end to everything. This period too came to an end.

One evening Johnny came in and told me that five more people and I had to be in Commandant Horst's office the following day at eight o'clock because they would take us from the hospital to the camp. He told me in secret that he chose this time to send me back to work because Horst had asked him who had been in the hospital for more than two weeks and, because he knew that the transport the next day was going to the neighbouring camp that had a good name, he put my name on the list. That was in the second part of December 1944.

The next day I was the first one in the office of that wild animal, Horst, because I wanted to be as far away as soon as possible. As Johnny told me, Horst was an orderly in an army hospital, a corporal. He volunteered to the SS, got the rank of sergeant and the opportunity to realise his sadistic leanings, lording over the doctors and deciding over life and death. He came to the office and saw that two men were not there yet. One of them came in on his heels and got a slap in the face that sent him flying to the wall. He sent for the last man, told us to stand in a row and commenced his speech. He was a lean, tall man of around fifty, I thought, with a Hitler moustache and malevolent eyes, and you saw that he enjoyed every second of his glory.

'You, Jewish swine, you think that you are in a sanatorium in a hospital and can get medicines as German soldiers do, but I'll take care of you, don't worry, we don't need parasite Jewish swine here!' With that he took the orderly, bent him over the table and told me to hold his head down. I said that I had no strength, so he called another man and each one of us got ten strokes with his crooked walking stick that this pride and joy of the German medical corps did not let out of his hand. I got another one, 'for strength'. Eventually we left for the camp of Wüstegiersdorf.

This camp was one of the best, as camps go. It was located in a big building and there were five hundred or so prisoners there. There were eight big rooms with more than thirty double-decked beds in each one. In the middle of every room there was a small iron stove that was not enough to heat the big room, but you could sit around it, warm yourself and try to dry the wet clothes after work.

A few lucky ones who worked in the potato depot could steal some potatoes and cook them in the evening, while the rest of us sat around and enjoyed the smell with hungry eyes. The fact that they could cook their potatoes without being torn to pieces by the others shows that in this camp the hunger was less terrible than in other camps. We got not a quarter, but a third, of the bread loaf and some people who worked in the central potato depot ate their fill there, and some potatoes trickled into the camp too. These lucky people exchanged some of the potatoes for cigarettes that those other prisoners who worked in a military bomb factory got once a week. These prisoners were the aristocrats of the camp as they got a special soup in their workplace. There were some minor drawbacks for them too: they got mercilessly pushed and three were shot for 'sabotage', but nevertheless some of them sold their portion of bread for sausages or margarine. There was warm water every evening in the shower room. That and the fact that they changed our underwear every two weeks meant that lice, the curse of the camps and of nearly all Germany at that time, were nearly unknown there.

Another big advantage of the camp was that all the capos and dignitaries, and the inmates too, were Hungarian Jews. The common language was an advantage, but the most important thing was that for us Hungarian Jews, this life in the camps had begun only a few months before so that the feelings of shame, solidarity and common fate were still alive amongst us, including the capos, to some extent. There was a 'Lager capo', that is the leader of capos, named Pinter, around thirty years old, compared to how our pyjamas looked like they were made for a scarecrow, his looked custom made and were always spic and span. People who knew him from home said that he was a pimp and had five women in his employ. I didn't know what he was at home, but here in camp he was the right man in the right place. He was a brave man, one who demands and gets respect and discipline without effort and who helped wherever he could. He saved hundreds of people from a certain and terrible end, as it will be seen in the next pages, and did it more than once. The rest of the capos were more or less human too, to the extent their dirty job allowed.

The source of this human behaviour was Grünberger 'bácsi', or Uncle Grünberger as everybody called him, who was the 'Lageraelteste' or the Jewish commandant of the camp. I knew him only a short time, but heard that he made sure that the capos did not beat and steal too much nor forgot where they came from. A short time before we arrived, an escapee from the camp who got caught in a neighbouring village was brought back and was to be hanged in the German style: the condemned has to stand on a low chair with the slipknot on his neck; they kick the chair under him and let him kick about until he chokes himself to death. As usual, they did it before the whole camp.

The commandant of the camp, an SS major, put the noose on the man's neck, held the usual speech which foretold the fate of anyone who tried to escape, and told Uncle Grünberger to kick the chair from under him. He refused to do it before the eyes of the whole camp, so the major had to do it himself. This refusal took incredible courage of Grünberger and that he was not hanged there with the condemned man was only because, as they said, he had friendly relations with the SS major (Obersturmbannfuerer). They said that this major was more human than the rest, but I am sure that if this incident had taken place two years earlier in 1942 when Germany was at the top of the world, Uncle Grünberger would have been hanged there and then. The SS majors were not chosen for their humanity.

The next morning we woke up to a rainy, windy, grey day but we knew that we were not in a bad place, as camps go. Before the counting I saw Johnny going somewhere near the office, ran to him to thank him again for everything he did for me and told him everything the hospital commandant, Horst, had said about not tolerating the 'parasite Jewish swine any longer.' Johnny hugged me and said that I had paid him back everything with that, because he had felt for a long time that something was going to happen, and if the patients in the hospital were taken back to Auschwitz for extermination, they would take the orderlies too, and therefore it would be safer for him to get a transfer to the camp soon. 'Our' major was from Austria too, like him, and within a few days I saw Johnny working in the clothes store.

We, the new ones who came from the hospital, were sent to the building project – Baukommando Lenz. The name of the project was 'Lenz', which means 'spring' in German, but the weather was 'winter'. We were working in an open, muddy field; there was a slow but steady rain, not enough to stop working but more than enough to penetrate the thin pyjamas in a short time. The foremen did not know what to do with us since there was no real work to be done in the mud.

All that did not help us much. The chief engineers urged the uniformed German foremen from Organisation Todt, who pushed the Polish foremen, who shouted at the capos, who in turn beat us. When the rain got heavier, we went into a leaky barrack where there was no place to sit, no escape from the rain and the standing around made the pangs of hunger even worse.

Azriel Feuerstein

It was Christmas already and it got colder and colder. Pinter, the Lager capo, went to the chief engineer and told him that there were letters in the camp by the Todt Organisation saying that there was no progress in the work because the people were lazy, but that in fact it was impossible for the people to work in this weather without gloves.

On Christmas day we got the day off, but the only other change was that we got gloves for work. In these difficult days, the only good thing was the warm water in the evenings that somehow helped to thaw the frozen limbs and the stove in the room, to sit around. In the days after the holidays we saw that the food seemed to get better. There were better soups with more potatoes and we got more sausage and margarine for the bread than usual. These were the first days of January 1945. On the still cold, wintry nights you could hear a kind of murmur from the east. It seemed that this murmur was getting nearer and there was talk about a Russian breakthrough at the front. On the one hand that gave us some hope of freedom soon, but on the other hand we feared that the Germans would finish us off at the last moment. In the end, neither happened. They took us into Germany before the Russians arrived.

14 January 1945. We did not go to work. They closed the gates. The capos told everyone to repair their shoes and the foot-clothes we wore instead of socks and get ready for a long march. First of all, my friend Tibi and I made an illegal pouch for bread in case we had the opportunity to steal some food while on the road. We wore it under the coat so that it would not be seen and stolen. In the evening, Johnny found me and took me to the clothes depot where he worked. He gave me a warmer coat, but tore it so that it would not seem too new, a warm shirt, pants, a brand new stomach warmer – I took one for Tibi too – and a pair of new socks that he told me to hide under the foot-cloth. He asked me if he should also change my underwear with some that had just come in from disinfection, which is delousing. I hesitated because just two days ago I had got clean ones, but in the end I changed them. He ran after me and gave me a woollen cap with

ear warmers that you wore under the ordinary cap, and that Tibi already had, and half a loaf of bread too. I knew that I would have no opportunity to return his kindness and only thanked him. I did not see Johnny again and I always hoped that he was able to hide somewhere and wait for the Russians. About the unforeseen and unlucky results of these many gifts, I had no foreboding at all.

The next day, 15 January 1945, had a promising beginning. We got hot and sweet coffee with milk, a big slice of bread with margarine and sausage. Half an hour later, after breakfast and the counting, we got an extra half bread for the way, and people who did not have a pouch for it were in trouble. The counting was short. The sentries stood on both sides of the marching body. They wore a warm and thick winter uniform, sweaters, a heavy overcoat and military raincoats and were armed of course, and we saw that there were hard days ahead of us. But who would have thought that we would look back with longing on these camps, which at the time we were sure were hell itself, when in fact the real hell and suffering had just began.

We did not know it, but on the same day all the camps from everywhere in the neighbourhood and on the fringes began to march toward inner Germany. The Germans did not want the Allied armies or the Russians to liberate these camps. To kill the inmates in the camps was not so simple. In those days, even the most fanatic SS officer saw that Hitler's victory wasn't very near, that they would have to account for their murders, and there just was not enough time to hide the traces of new murders. That is why they decided on the Death March of tens of thousands of Jews.

But we were not the only ones on the roads. They were full of fleeing Germans and their collaborators, who fled before the just vengeance of the local populations and the Russian Army. Trucks, taxis, personal cars, horse driven vehicles of all kinds, tractors, pushcarts, baby carriages, all were on their way westward, fleeing with whatever they had succeeded to pile on their vehicles. The 'Herrenvolk' knew that the Russians would make them pay for their crimes in the occupied territories. But in spite of all that, some of them still threw stones at us if they had enough energy left. From time to time, everybody, Jews and Germans too, had to get off the road, to make way for the tanks and trucks of Hitler's invincible army fleeing before the approaching Russians. These pictures, alas, we could not enjoy often, only at the crossroads, because they tried to lead us through the field-roads. But that came later, and for now we only knew that we were going. Where? In which direction? Why and for how long? We did not know.

With the beginning of the march, the snow too commenced to fall. The wet snow stuck to the soles of the shoes, and every step got more difficult. Tibi and I talked about the outings with the family in the winter snow until we got too tired to talk. This Tibi was a very close friend of mine. Ours was the kind of friendship that is common in wartime and danger, the kind of closeness that forms in a short moment but lasts a lifetime. There are not many days when I do not see his face before me, but his family name I have forgotten.

He was the son of a chemist from Nyiregyháza, whose father tried to escape from the Ghetto in Hungary and got trampled and kicked to death by the Hungarian gendarmes there. Tibi was my age, sixteen, somewhat taller than me, with a broad, smiling face that was not emaciated but rather somewhat swollen from hunger. We both got out from the hospital the same day and did not know each other before, but hit it off the first moment we saw each other. We did not work in the same place, but he slept on the bed above me. When there were cold nights he came down and we slept together, covering ourselves with all the blankets. He sometimes brought me one potato from where he was working and I got for him a stomach–warmer, my old overcoat, and gave him half the bread I got from Johnny.

In the camp there was not much time for talking but now we always marched together. What did we talk about? Food, like everybody else, but there was not much strength for talking. At the beginning of the march they told us that anyone who leaves the unit without permission or can't continue gets shot. Our capos made us hurry because every evening there was a destination where we were to sleep and which we had to reach, however long it took. The march got more and more difficult. The wet clothes and their weight did not make things easier. There was half an hour rest at twelve o'clock, without soup, so we ate the bread. Only the first ones got a half hour rest, while those who came later had to be on their way again after some minutes. The only good thing was the small pile of turnips for the nearby cattle. Tibi stood up to pee and covered me while I stole two turnips and put them in our pouch, which helped us in the next days.

After the rest we got up again and it was not easy. At least, while walking, you got warmer, but the clothes remained wet. We had no strength for talk, only to move our feet. We got to a crossroad and continued straight ahead, but in the ditch by the roadside I saw a bundle of blue-white pyjamas, like ours. I looked closer and saw the blood. It was a prisoner, shot. It must have been someone from a camp that went ahead of us. Skin and bones, and there was nobody to close his terrified eyes. That was the first person we saw who was killed on the march, but not the last one. We hurried on.

There was a thin cover of snow on the frozen earth, but when the snowing ceased it got even colder. The sun emerged suddenly from the clouds and continued its way westwards. At last we arrived at a huge cowshed with only a few cows in it.

They left some soldiers with us to make sure we did not light a fire to warm ourselves. The cooks made some warm coffee and it poured some strength into our weary bones. We were hungry and our clothes and shoes were wet. I was mostly worried about the shoes because I was afraid that the wounds on my ankles would reopen, which actually happened later.

I had a new, up to now unknown, problem too: an itching in my groin and armpits that I had not felt before. If I had not known that I got underclothes just the day before, straight from disinfection, I would have suspected lice. I was very tired and did not have much time to think, so I went to sleep under the wet blankets.

Azriel Feuerstein

The next day, the second day of the march, the weather was clear and cold. We got no food but the cooks made some black coffee with sugar, and if you drank it fast you could get another portion. I wanted to eat our bread but Tibi, who was more deliberate and thrifty, said that we had to think about tomorrow, so we ate the cattle-turnip I had succeeded in stealing the day before. The cooks who had a horse-drawn cart with the products got started before us. They were in better condition than we and the plan was that they should arrive before us to have time to prepare something to eat for midday, and the same in the evening. The food on the cart was chiefly for the SS.

What can you write about marching in the snow, in leaden rain which froze on your clothes, with aching feet, driven and beaten all the way, under the sway of the stomach-tearing hunger? You bend your head, see the heels of the man before you, you stumble and slip without end. It was hard on everyone, but for me it was harder because of the itching that got worse over time. I put my hand under my armpit and drew out a couple of young, healthy and seemingly happy lice. I was not only very uncomfortable from the itching but very much ashamed too. As I wrote before, in the camp, which we had left only two days ago, there was warm water every evening and so lice were nearly unknown. I told my problem to Tibi and we came to the conclusion that the underclothes I got from Johnny had not been disinfected as they should have been, perhaps because of the hurry before leaving the camp. Tibi inspected the stomach warmer I got for him and he too found some unwanted aliens. I don't know if it was because of the unfinished disinfections, or because we slept together under the same blankets. It is certain that Johnny wanted to do me a favour, but the result certainly could have been better.

We discussed what to do against the lice and came to the conclusion that I had to take off my underclothes, lay them on the snow and try to clean the seams from the lice and their eggs. We arrived at a big but empty silo. The soldiers slept in the houses of the families where they got fed. The two soldiers who stayed to supervise us were changed every two hours, but they too trembled from cold in spite of their warm clothes. We, without anything to eat or drink, did our best not to freeze to death and embraced to warm each other. At least the others did, because Tibi and I had a project. We sought out a half-open corner, with clean snow powder. I took off my clothes, spread them on the snow, covered myself with the three wet blankets and commenced to clean up the seams that were the dwelling places of the lice and their eggs. After a short time, we realised that even if we destroyed most of them, there would still remain enough eggs for the future generations, but that if I remained naked for ten more minutes, I would perish on the spot. So, in spite of Tibi urging me to wait a bit longer, I put on my cold, wet and lousy underwear and clothes and what a delight it was! I nearly said that I got warm. Everything is relative.

The next morning the cooks prepared some kind of soup from the vegetables that the Lager capo Pinter bought, begged for and stole, and in it, with some luck, you could find even bits of potatoes. Our hunger reached such a degree that to have eaten one's fill was unknown and, after eating, you were only more aware of the hunger. However, in spite of that we got on our way feeling better. After marching for some hours, Tibi asked for permission to step aside, and got it after the guard warned the one behind him. After a minute Tibi came back running and holding his belly. It turned out that from the corner of his eye he had seen laying in the grass by the side of the road a big cattle turnip that had fallen off a passing van and had run to pick it up. That was very lucky because our pouch was empty in spite of Tibi's thriftiness. Some time before the lunch break, we heard the sound of a shot being fired from the end of the column that was far away. There was no need for explanations since we knew that somebody was unable to continue and the SS had shot him. He was the first one from our camp.

It was late when we came to our sleeping place, and got nothing to eat or drink this time because nobody allowed the cooks to use their fireplace. At least the sleeping quarter was better: full of clean smelling hay. I persuaded Tibi that we should take off our shoes and foot clothes for the night to let them dry. Tibi was afraid that somebody might steal them and that would be a death sentence. Of course, he was right, and later we took our shoes off only when we were awake. This one time, some good came out of it in spite of everything; Tibi thought about the shoes all night, woke up before anyone and found a horse fodder sack half full with oats that belonged to the peasant, and stole as much as he dared. A bit of luck because we woke up with an empty belly, and that is how we went on our way too. We rubbed the oats in our hands till the prickly skin was halfway off and chewed the grains. It gave the teeth something to do.

The weather got better. The sun came out and it seemed that it was not as cold as before, but there were a few for whom it was too late. After a couple of hours of marching, we began to hear shots from the end of the column; first only from time to time, but later more often. That meant that there were more 'Mussulmans'. This was a term in the camps, which meant people who were still on their feet, like the rest of the walking skeletons, but if you looked into their eyes you saw that the life was missing. In a minute or an hour they would fall down, dead. Why were they called Mussulmans? Perhaps because of the real Mussulmans supposed fatalism. It is enough to say that there were very few of that sort who came back to the land of the living. The fact that there were more Mussulmans around did not bode well for the rest of us who were still in a somewhat better condition.

Tibi and I, chewing the oats, found ourselves nearly at the head of the column, in spite of the lessons I learned in Auschwitz never to be between the first or the last ones, etc. This time the lunch break was near a big barn. The cooks with the cart were still there and we saw that the horse was at the end of his tether and wouldn't be able to draw the cart or his life much longer. Pinter, the Lager capo, told the major that it would perhaps be best to parcel out the bread there and then.

Under the covers on the cart there were some two hundred loaves of bread that they planned to give us a few days later when we met the train that would take us farther, but Pinter said that if we waited any longer, we would have neither the horse, nor the people to draw the cart and so the major decided that everyone would get half a loaf, with the warning that there was no more and wouldn't be more till the end of the march. Tibi decided that we'd eat half the bread then, and put away the other half away for later. The eating part was easy, the putting away part much harder.

I don't remember where we spent that night or how, but I know that in spite of all the good intentions we began the fifth day of the march with an empty pouch, an empty stomach and with the very bad feeling that it would take a long time until we'd get something to eat. That was exactly what happened, and we did not find anything to steal either or, as it was called in the camps, 'organise'.

The shots from the end of the column got nearer and more frequent. It began to snow again and on the muddy road every step was more painful than the one before it. The wet clothes made it even worse. We went to sleep wet, weary and in pain and that is how we woke up until the sixth and even the seventh day of marching. The only difference was that there was more shooting from the end and that we left eight dead men in the morning. I said to the peasant that he should leave them, as, in a few days, he too would have to flee before the Russians. He looked at me and did not break my head, which was nice of him, even if at that time and place it would not have made much difference to me.

We got on our way and had to stop before the usual lunch hour. The poor horse passed away. Pinter convinced the SS officer that the horse was still alive and had to be slaughtered immediately. The soldiers were hungry too and nobody came to feel the horse's pulse. Among the cooks there was a butcher from home who slaughtered the dead horse like the expert he was. The best part went to the SS as steaks and from the rest of it they cooked a thick soup for us with the remaining potatoes and vegetables. The only problem with the soup was that we had to eat it without bread. We were near a forester's lodge with a huge shed and there was enough brushwood around for a big fire. It was late so we slept over there.

The next morning, we woke up earlier than usual. We had kept the fire burning the whole night so that it would not be too cold. We got coffee and the rest of the soup from the day before which they had diluted a bit. We ate and got on our way with something in our belly for a change. It seems that, in spite of its appearance, that little horse was a racehorse because, after some time, we, and the SS too, began to run around to the wayside and gave back the horse to the good earth where it belonged in various ways. Even worse, the soldiers got orders that we had to reach the sleeping place, however long it took. The cart was without the horse so it had to be drawn. We got to the shed late, hungry and tired and that was also the way we woke up to the ninth day of the march.

We got on our way after leaving nine dead in the shed and from the beginning the sound of shots was our steady companion. I, in my stupid way, go on and speak about the sound of shots and forget there are perhaps people who might think that I speak about hunter's shots or shots fired in joy. No, my friends, these shots were fired by the SS sergeant to kill those who were unable to continue. He even complained that his gun did not have time to cool off and that it was very difficult to kick all those dead bodies into the wayside ditch. He also explained that they were not only dirty Jews, but 'Mussulmans' too, and it was an act of mercy to spare them the long drawn out process of dying. That is the way Lucifer explains his ways in Goethe's Faust: 'I am a part of that Force that always wants to do the Bad, but does the Good.'

It was some days since Tibi and I had set our eyes on a tall lanky boy, around our age, by the name of Nadler Tomi. Tomi was an intelligent and nice boy, from a very rich and well-known family from Budapest. He wore a blanket on his shoulder like each one of us. But what a blanket! Most of the blankets were half rotten, old military ones. There were some civilian blankets too, but not like Tomi's. His was thick, all wool, with bright green patterns on a background that must have been white once that could be seen from far away. It was the king of blankets. At

151

this stage of the march there were enough blankets to go around. So many were dead that everybody who wanted to could exchange his old blankets for something better or take a second one, if it was not too heavy for him to carry. But of course, not a blanket like Tomi's. In the past few days we had seen that Tomi was in the last stages. And don't think that we wanted to take away his blanket. What were we, animals? Simply, when he fell down, as he would in a few minutes or hours, it would be such a waste to leave him by the wayside with the blanket. When we saw that his steps were aimless and that he began to fall behind, we took him in the middle between us to help him and Tibi said that we should take the blanket only when he fell down. Of course, Tibi and I discussed all that between us two, with Tomi between us, as there was no fear to hurt his feelings, as he was a "Mussulman" who did not hear or feel anything. He liked our help and took our elbow so as not to stumble. Bad luck: he did not fall down but stayed on his feet all evening. We said that we would seek him first thing in the morning if he were still alive.

Before continuing to write, I sat for some five minutes thinking about how to describe that night, which was one of the two worst nights of this terrible period and, I hope and pray, of my whole life. Just before darkness we arrived, weak, weary, hungry and deadly tired to a big, closed barn full with fresh smelling hay. The hay was on both sides of a five-metre wide concrete way, with a metre high wall on both sides.

They drove us in and let us stand on this concrete way that could not have been longer than fifteen to twenty metres. There remained some five hundred of us as one hundred had already died. We stood there pressed together. There was no place to sit and we only wanted to get up to that hay and close our eyes.

The SS ate and drank something and got on that wall together with the capos. They brought in some six hundred Ukrainian girls and led them to the hay on both sides of the way. The girls had twenty armed female SS guards who sat on both sides of the wall, and said that anyone who tried to climb on the wall they would shoot without warning. Our SS left and shut the doors. It was pitch dark inside, as we stood pressed together without being able to move. People screamed. The horse from yesterday had not finished its cleaning functions yet and, if somebody squatted down, he had a good chance of being trampled to death. You had to piss too - the night was cold - and you could do it in your own pants or on the pants of the one before you. In the middle of the night I suddenly felt a hand on my head and somebody snatched away my cap with the ear warmers; without thinking I stretched out my hand and snatched away somebody else's cap. After having written this down, I read it and do not understand what was so terrible about that night. Believe me, it was terrible.

After a night without end, at last came a morning. First thing, we sought our patient from the day before. The colours of that blanket shouted from far away. It seems that Tomi had found a bit of barbed wire somewhere and wound it around him and the blanket. He saw us and fled. What happened to him? We only wanted to help.

But now we had other worries: how to survive the next few hours. It was the tenth day of marching and after the tiring, sleepless night and the tearing hunger, it was not easy to lift one's feet and put them down again. Tibi was in no better condition either. After three hours we came to a railway in the middle of nowhere. We sat down and waited. We sat on a rock, near a low wire fence of single strands. Between the rock and the fence there was a shallow ditch which went in the direction of a feeding place for cattle some thirty metres inside the fence, where three cows fed from a feeding trough. Tibi sat so as to cover me somewhat and I crouched, lifted the lowest strand of the barbed wire with a stick, crawled to the trough, filled my shirt and pockets with cattle turnip and crawled back, without being detected. After me there were some others who tried it too. The last one was seen and shot

In the meantime a truck came and with it the major. He had left his horse in the city and in the truck he brought some products for the SS and for us too. We got a quarter of bread for a journey that lasted four days, instead of the planned one day. We were able to put some of the turnips away in the pouch, but the bread we devoured at once.

The train arrived too but we were still waiting. This train consisted of open freight wagons with a closed one at the end for the SS. After one more hour, we saw a ragged column of prisoners nearing: the group we were waiting for. They were not more than a hundred, but from the number of their guards you saw that they were at least four times more when they had begun marching. If we thought ourselves to be near the end of our tether, compared with this group we were prizefighters. They were clad in torn and dirty summer pyjamas and nearly fell down at every step. The last one crawled on all fours and the SS sergeant lashed him to make him crawl faster. Some steps before the train, when that unlucky man thought that he had at last arrived at the Promised Land, the sergeant shot him, saying, 'He would have been unable to climb onto the train, anyway.' Even our guard turned away in disgust.

We climbed into the open wagons. They pressed in some seventy people in each one and the new sergeant remarked that anyone who did not feel comfortable could continue on foot. In our wagon, by chance, there were some of the new group and they sat down near us at the wagon's side. We chose the side because we thought that it was something to lean on. We thought too that, however bad these open wagons were, they could not be worse than marching. The difference was like choosing between cholera and typhus. It began to rain: rain mixed with snow and within a few minutes, rivulets began to flow down the wall of the wagon straight into our necks. We tried to hold a blanket above our heads, but it flew into our sleeves, and the blanket became a water-basin. We were hungry too but knew we would be unable to keep the turnips that I stole to ourselves, so we gave the new ones some and the rest we ate at once and were greatly relieved.

The new prisoners knew that we spoke Hungarian, so they chose to speak Polish and we couldn't understand. The shoes of one of them were not too bad, but the other one's were in pieces so that he wore the foot clothes on top of his shoes and had to bind them with bits of wire. His friend calmed him by saying that

Azriel Feuerstein

I would die soon and then they would take my shoes away. I understood from their conversation that they would not bother to bring a doctor to see if I was really dead. The Slovak dialect around my hometown, Kassa, is very much similar to Polish so I understood every word. After some hearty swearing from my part, they accepted the fact that they'd have to wait a bit with the changing of the shoes and we got quite friendly. They came from Camp Dörnau, which was called a Labour Camp but in fact was more an extermination camp. They did not kill people with gas there, but with slow starvation to death. It seems that the people who were selected in Wolgsberg, whom I saw in that open truck from my scaffolding, were not taken to Auschwitz but to Dörnau and thus I acquired my fear of heights on false presumptions. Nevertheless, up to this day, if I look down from the second storey, I must hold onto something. On the other hand, gas or no gas, nearly all of those who were selected starved to death there.

It got dark. Let's not forget that we are talking about nighttime at the end of January in Upper Silesia, the middle of Europe. I did not have my thermometer with me, but it was cold enough for our clothes to freeze on our bodies. Hell's inferno seemed a place we'd prefer.

In the meantime, the traffic above our head was continuous. Hundreds of aeroplanes flew over us day and night. They were heavy bombers that bombed Hanover: the British by day and the Americans by night. Our new companion, the one with the good shoes, died and we heaved him out of the wagon, not without exchanging his shoes with the shoeless one, who was able to enjoy them for only two days before we heaved him out too. On the second day, they stopped the train at noon. We stood a couple of kilometres before Hanover. Even from that distance we could smell the stink and see the flames of the burning city that was ground to dust by the bombings of the last months. The train could not continue and we felt some satisfaction when we saw the heroic SS spring out of their wagon and run to the nearby trees every half an hour when there were aeroplanes over us. This satisfaction did not, alas, make the tearing hunger any better. On the other hand, our wagon was getting comfortable as we had thrown out nearly twenty bodies.

The next day our train began to move, but not more than half an hour later an aeroplane circled us and strafed the closed wagon of the SS, without shooting at the open wagons. It seemed that the pilot saw that they were full of prisoners and guessed that the closed one was for the guards. We discovered later that the SS had lost only two men, bad luck, one of which was 'our' major. We would have greatly preferred it to be the new sergeant, but it was better than nothing.

The train stopped at the station of Bergen-Belsen. Up to now we had not heard the name of that camp. Right there, at the station, we began to smell the disgusting sweet stink of dead bodies that got stronger as we got nearer to the camp. It was the smell of unburied bodies. Please, bring to me the Germans from the neighbourhood, who said that they did not know what was happening in the camp and let me spit in their eyes. It was impossible not to be aware of that smell from many kilometres and impossible not to know what caused it.

We got on our way from the station to the camp, one or two kilometres away on a low hill. As we approached the gate of the camp the smell got steadily stronger, and we saw that here even the capos were skin and bones.

The last ones before the gate gathered their last ounces of strength to get in as the sergeant lashed them and promised to shoot the last one. An SS officer, who they said was the commander of the camp, Kremer's deputy, joked loudly that they should take pictures of these skeletons making their way on all fours to get into the camp to show the world how the Jews love Bergen-Belsen.

Our Lager capo, Pinter, whose clothes even then, after all we had been through, looked as if freshly pressed, went to this animal, standing at attention Prussian style, and reported that his men had not had any food for more than four days. I saw the shocked reaction of the guard at this unimaginable presumption that a Jew should speak to an SS officer without being spoken to first. The sergeant from Dornau took his gun and we were all sure that it was the end of Pinter. But the officer, from astonishment I think, ordered that they should give us something to eat. We got some foul smelling soup that tasted heavenly after the last four days of starvation, and coffee too.

They told us to sit down around the Appelplatz where the counting was nearly finished and, after 'dismiss', there remained eight skeletons. The only difference between them and those who were still able to drag themselves back to the barrack was a diminishing sparkle of life.

Two men came into the empty Appelplatz with pushcarts and shovel and you could see that it was a regular service after every counting. They put the dead men on the pushcart, and with the shovel put the other garbage on top of it and took it to a big hole.

The man with the pushcart came around to the last body and you could see that he was deadly tired. With the last ounces of his strength, he heaved the last skeleton, which was once, however difficult it was to believe, a man just like you and I, on the pushcart, and got on his way. Suddenly, the incredible happened: the dead man sat up in the pushcart. The cleaner stopped to think a bit and then took the shovel and whacked his passenger on the head. He fell back and returned to his natural and proper state. The truth is that I understood the man with the pushcart very well. What else could he do? Dump him? The Appelplatz had to be clean. He chose the only possible and logical solution for that time and place, so don't blame him but blame the time and place and the men who made that happen.

These moments are deeply and clearly engraved in my mind. They stand clean and sharp before my eyes: the deadly tired pushcart man; the barely moving dead man; the shovel. That was the first, and however incredible it sounds, the last time I felt that I was going to die.

At the same time, the commandant of the camp, SS Obersturmbannführer Kremer, walked past with his big wolfhound, which he called 'Mensch' (that means *man*). When he wanted him to catch a prisoner, he told him: 'Man, catch the dog!' Such a droll man, I beg your pardon, SS!

Our Lager capo Pinter now neared this vicious animal with military marching steps, stopped three metres away, took his cap off and stood to attention. It seems that the SS officer was so astonished that he didn't think to set his dog on Pinter. Pinter stood there without stirring and, after Kremer asked him what he wanted, he said that he had heard that they wanted people for work and, since his group had just arrived and were ready for work, he asked they be sent. Kremer asked how many people were in his group. Without waiting for an answer he was ordered to take the men into the nearby barrack and the following day to select from them four hundred people for work. He turned on his heels and returned to his office. Anyone who was not there cannot appreciate Pinter's incredible courage in approaching a man like Kremer, who set his hound on people for much lesser offences. With this act Pinter saved, or at least prolonged, the life of four hundred men.

Everybody ran to the barrack. In our group there were some four hundred and fifty men, but others, who heard that there was a possibility of leaving Bergen-Belsen, did their best to get in. This barrack was a big empty room that could hold some three hundred or so, but five hundred got in. We sat down into each other.

That was the second worst night of my life. I am unable to describe the pictures, the feelings, the horrors, the sickening disgust and despair of that night. My words are unable to do it, and even Dante, who described hell, would stand speechless before that sight. The windows were closed, the door was locked. Outside there were SS patrols with dogs trained to kill. The air was as thick as pea soup. After some hours, when it got truly unbearable, Tibi intended to stand up and break the window for some fresh air, but I did not let him because if he stood up, he would not be able to sit down again. Instead of that, we put the two mess tins in the pouch and Tibi, who was sitting under the window, heaved it up and down, until he broke the window and it gave at least the illusion of some fresh air.

Among the strangers, who had been in the camp longer and had somehow got in, there were a few with typhus. These men were unable to restrain themselves and did it in their cap or mess tin and threw the result away into the room, the farther the better. It was not only disgusting, but the man who was hit by that missile was in deadly danger, because he wouldn't stand a chance in the selection for work the next day when you had to seem clean and strong. After an eternity there was light and somehow I got out, in spite of the patrols and the dogs. I took off my shirt, washed myself and even got back into the barrack unharmed. It seems that in the meantime a patrol had passed the door and left a man with a broken head near it.

After some hours they began the selection for work. Tibi and I stood near the door in order to be among the first ones. The selected ones they sent into the opposite barrack and those who were not selected stayed outside. The selection was conducted by the fat (everything is relative) capo, justly hated by everyone, and that is why Pinter gave him the job. Tibi was selected at once, but not I. He wanted to stay with me, but I did not allow it, since it would not have helped me anyway.

I climbed in through the window, but that swine of a capo saw me and threw me out. It was my luck that Pinter came to tell him something, and while the capo was occupied, I slunk in through the door. Tibi greeted me in tears. At the last counting, we were four hundred and one. One was left behind in Bergen-Belsen. Not me. We heard that we were going to Hildesheim.

15

Tomi and the Blanket

'Hey, Yeory, a new suit I see. What elegance! You look very well,' exclaimed Fröken Ulle.

'God Dag, Fröken Ulle, it is really very nice of you to come to visit, even today near the end of the Passover holiday, as I am sure that you have a lot of work to do. What do you say, not only did they find me a jacket in my size, but I even got a pair of shoes my size in this land of big feet,' I cheerfully replied.

'The pants seem a bit too long. I'll talk with the girls and perhaps somebody can shorten them,' replied Fröken Ulle.

'Thank you, but it is not necessary. In the evening I am going to visit the Hungarian girls in the barracks near the lake as there are some seamstresses from home, and I am sure that somebody will help me.'

As for the new suit: the Flyktlings Büro, the office for foreign refugees, had invited me along with every other refugee to a central store to give us new suits for the summer.

'Come here, Yeory, let's sit down and drink our coffee. As you said, the holidays are coming to an end, and I have a lot of questions about the last chapter.

'For example, I am unable to understand the indifference about the death of that man who was in the same bed as you in the hospital, or when you speak about how your friend Johnny "helped" that man, who was operated on for appendicitis, to pass away. Or that capo, Pinter, whom you admire and revere, was it really necessary to write that at home he was a gigolo and had five women working for him? And who was that lanky boy with you today?'

THE TUMBLER

I asked, 'If you saw us, Fröken Ulle, why did you not come down? You would have had a very nice surprise. About the other questions: as they say, *one who was not there cannot understand it*. We, who lived through it, use this morbid, cynical mode of speech with survivors' pride. Without that it would be impossible to speak about those times. It was not easy to lie in the same bed as a dying man, and it was only natural that I felt relieved when he passed away. Of course, there was more space in the bed too.

'Excuse me for being cynical. After the operation, that poor man howled from pain the whole time after that swine of a sergeant gave orders not to give him painkillers. Since the doctor wanted to give him some anyway, if Johnny had not "helped" him, the sergeant would have shot the doctor and who knows whom else in his rage, and the man would have died anyway.

'Lastly, about Pinter, the fact that before the war he was a gigolo made his heroism and daring in the camps only more admirable in my eyes.'

'But was it really necessary to speak so much about the lice? Reading about it, I was itching all over; and all those disgusting descriptions about human excretions and incontinence!'

'All these things together, while evoking an uneasy feeling in the reader, help to explain the premeditated dehumanisation, this planned process, not only to exterminate you, but in the course of killing, to humiliate you too, to make you subhuman and dirty even in your own eyes, to show even to yourself how necessary and just this killing was.

'Is there anything more humiliating for a grown man than the fact that he is unable to contain himself? When I speak about those matters, I try to explain things, not only for the reader, but for myself too.'

'I didn't like the story about the unfortunate boy and his blanket that you intended to rob. Perhaps you know what happened to him?' Fröken Ulle asked.

'You too would know, Fröken Ulle if, instead of lurking about in the windows upstairs, you had come down. Like I said, you would have had a nice surprise. That tall boy you saw from the window was Nadler Tomi, the boy with the blanket.'

'Well, I am sorry that I did not come down, but tell me, what happened?' asked a very interested Fröken Ulle.

'Well, I am standing there trying on the suit and near me stands a tall boy whom I was sure I knew from somewhere. I asked him if he knew where we had met. He looked at me piercingly and said, "Of course, I know. You and your friend wanted to steal my blanket." And he said that in a loud voice, before everyone. I was so ashamed that I wanted to disappear. Then he hugged me and thanked me, saying we saved his life.'

A quizzical look came over Fröken Ulle's face as she asked, 'Now, really, I beg your pardon? How exactly did you save his life by wanting to steal his blanket?'

I defensively replied, 'Try to understand. Tomi was already a corpse, a living dead, a "Mussulman", who had lost his connection with the outside world. One moment or one hour and he would have fallen down, or dropped behind and had been shot by the SS sergeant. In some way, that even I don't understand, Tibi and I helped him to stay on his feet. He knew that we would take his blanket when he died, and this penetrated the fog in his brain and gave him the will to live, and this living dead began to plan. He wound a bit of barbed wire about him and his blanket, saw us, fled and so returned to the land of the living. Yes, we saved his life, and I am very glad for that. Of course, the blanket, I regret a bit.'

'Yeory, you would do it again!' exclaimed Fröken Ulle.

What do you say? She begins to understand jokes at first hearing. They will arrest me for un-Swedish activities and undermining the national character.

'Tell me, Yeory, and for once let us speak earnestly: when you speak in your usual cynical manner about the man with the pushcart who whacked that skeleton on the head, you mention that it was the first and last time in the camps that you felt that you could die there. Is it true? There, where death was around you everywhere, you really did not feel before or after that you would die there?' asked an interested Fröken Ulle.

'It is good that you ask, Fröken Ulle,' I replied, 'It is true and I wrote it down without thinking. Now, when I think about it, I cannot explain it, but it is true. Like a Jew, I'll answer a question with a question: how is it possible that our constant topic of conversation was how we would meet our family, our parents, after all we had seen and heard? These questions are waiting for a psychologist to be answered. Only once did I feel again that I would die, and it was after the liberation. I'll tell you about it when we get that far in my story.'

'Yes, Yeory, but not now, because I must run. You look very good in your new suit. Wear it in good health, and goodbye,' said Fröken Ulle.

'Goodbye, and thank you for everything,' I replied.

16

Hildesheim and Bergen-Belsen Again

The journey from Bergen-Belsen took a long time. We were taken in closed wagons so it did not rain in, and there were less people in the wagon than before, but the pain of the hunger ate our insides. The only food we had got in the last four days was that soup at the gate of Bergen-Belsen. I was sure of one thing: nothing could be worse than in there. Both Tibi and I were very glad that we remained together and hoped that, therefore, we would have a better chance of surviving what was to come.

At last, we were in Hildesheim. In our state of hunger we were not in the mood to appreciate the beauties of the surroundings. However, I saw that we had come to a city, the kind of which not many remained in Germany at that time as, by February 1945, most towns and cities were in ruins from the unceasing bombings. Here at the station, we saw some signs of bombings but the town itself, as far as we could see, had seemed untouched since the Middle Ages. Here, on both sides of the streets, there were small houses, some of which sunk into the earth up to their window sills with an inscription in Gothic letters and numbers, 'Built in 1352'. Such a house was on the other side of our temporary home that was a not so long ago an abandoned Variety, as the torn placards showed. They had taken out the seats both downstairs and upstairs, filled them with straw mattresses and put two blankets on each one. Much more important, even before going in, everyone got a third of a bread, and no one can describe the heavenly taste of that black, mud-like bread that we swallowed reverently and in tears, because who knew when we would get some again.

THE TUMBLER

The nights in those abandoned rooms with high ceilings were ice-cold and, even sleeping together, Tibi and I were unable to get warm. In the morning, we felt better because we got hot coffee and a piece of bread. After a short alarm and the counting, we were led to the railway station where our work was to repair and change the railway lines that got damaged during the bombings.

As I mentioned before, Hildesheim is some thirty kilometres away from Hanover, a big and important city and a railway centre of strategic importance and, as such, it was under unceasing bombings. In spite of the fact that a lot of people were evacuated to the surrounding villages, many people still lived in the city and they had to have their daily food and fuel. It was clear that the railway there was a primary target for the bombers. The problem of supplies was solved by sending the trains to Hildesheim and from there by trucks to Hanover because the highways were not as heavily bombed.

The British tried to bomb the station in Hildesheim once a week, usually on Tuesdays. The Americans bombed Hanover at night, and the British by day, every time with an armada of two to three hundred planes. From these armadas the British sent four to five planes to Hildesheim once a week to bomb the trains, the railway approaching the station and chiefly the small bridge which they usually missed. They brought us here from Bergen-Belsen to repair and exchange the damaged rails. This work was usually finished by Sunday, on Monday the Germans brought in some trains, on Tuesday the British bombed again, and so everybody was satisfied: the British, because they damaged the station again; the Germans, because they brought in some supplies for Hanover; and we because there was new work for us to do, which meant they wouldn't take us back to the death camp.

We had two additional reasons for being thankful: one of them was the nearly daily air-raid alert. As I said, they bombed Hanover and to do it they flew over Hildesheim. Even when they did not bomb, the alert had to be sounded because the SS did not want to be put in danger. At every alert we had to climb the nearby cemetery hill. Hildesheim, like many medieval cities, was built around a hill. At the top of the hill was the church, around it the cemetery and the city lay around the hill. That is how I remember it and, if I am wrong, I am sorry, but it was a long time ago. The cemetery was a nice, friendly place on sunny days and even on rainy ones, and we preferred to be with dead Germans rather than with living ones. It was also nice to rest.

The other reason for satisfaction was the bombed wagons in the station. It was I who made this discovery. On the very first morning when we came to work, I smelled burning sugar. I saw one of the bombed wagons dripping into a puddle. I ran with my mess tin and dipped it into the puddle. It is true that, beside the sweetened rainwater, there was some mud too, but what a taste!

Later I learned not to dip my tin too deep in and then with less mud it tasted even better, not that we minded it too much. Even the taste of the grease from the wagon wheels we did not mind much, at least not in the beginning.

Later we grew bolder and saw that there were half opened wagons with sugar nearly untouched by fire and we filled our pockets, even though we knew that touching it meant a death sentence for plundering.

Once, when we came down after a bombing, we saw a damaged wagon that was full of wooden boxes, and in every one ten round cheeses, faintly smelling of sweating feet. Tibi hid one under his coat, and the guards should have found it by the smell, but they did not, because we all smelled the same, and not of roses.

These cheeses were hard and called 'quargel' and, as one connoisseur explained, when ready they get squashy, smell much stronger and are eaten with beer. For me, they were smelly enough even so, but we ate them in two days. After the war, I was not satisfied until I tasted this cheese as it should be eaten, with a bottle of beer, and it was quite tasty, but for a few hours afterwards I smelled so bad that everyone gave me a wide berth.

One day a group, with Tibi among them, was taken to a bombed chocolate factory to help put out a fire. He came back happy and with a wide smile because they ate chocolate the whole day. He pulled me aside and took out a big chunk of chocolate, don't ask me where from, and gave it to me. It was pure happiness.

I think that it happened on 10 March 1945. For some days we had felt that some change was in the air because of the behaviour of the guards. The shouting and the blasphemies were more subdued, and they were discussing something with gloomy faces. I said to Tibi that either they had got an order to shoot us or they had been told they were to go to the Russian Front, which got nearer every day. I was partly right.

That morning, after the counting, the guards did not place themselves as usual on either side of our group, but stayed as a unit on one side with their sergeant at the head. A group of 'Volkssturm' marched in through the gate. These consisted of men under sixteen and over sixty years of age, and were the trash of the German Army who were conscripted at the very end of the war. Now, in these days, when the regular soldiers gave themselves up to the British and the Americans, Hitler used them to prolong the war for a few more days.

These soldiers now marching in were clad either in motley WWI uniforms, or in short pants of the Hitler-Jugend and wore armbands with the swastika. Many of them were old and we saw it as a good omen because we thought that they knew the times before Hitler, and we hoped that they were less fanatic than the young. They certainly wouldn't be worse than the SS, we thought. Incredibly, we were wrong: they were worse, even the old ones.

Their leader, an old prick from WWI, with a crooked walking stick, a Hitler- moustache, and full of self-importance called, if I remember right, Gruber, ordered, 'Attention!' to his unit. He marched in the familiar German goose-steps to the SS sergeant, who nearly exploded trying to restrain his guffawing, and relieved him from the guard. The sergeant led the SS guards, in goose-steps too, out of the gate – a thing they definitely had not done in the last few years - and we heard them laugh themselves sick. *OK*, I thought to myself, *at the Russian Front you won't have much to laugh about.*

Azriel Feuerstein

In spite of the fact that we saw who Gruber was, we too had to try hard not to laugh. Gruber gave us an introductory speech in which every second word was 'Saujuden', that is Jewish swine, and the gist of it was that we wouldn't have much to laugh about and enjoy life. In that he was right. As a punishment, he led us to work running, but they got tired faster than we, and that made Gruber even angrier. He wanted to interfere in work too, tried to beat everyone with his crooked walking stick, howled 'los, los' and wanted fewer of us to lift and replace the heavy rails. At last it got to be too much and the foreman, the meister, who was a railway worker from before the war, called the chief engineer who took Gruber aside, and explained to him that his responsibility was the guard and that he should not interfere with work, so he ceased.

When the daily air raid sounded, Gruber wanted the Jews to remain at the station because, if they died, nobody would regret it and the chief engineer agreed at once. He only said that in that case, the guard soldiers should stay with them, which Gruber's unit did not greet with enthusiasm. He was lucky because the railway workers said that they were forbidden to remain at their post when there was an alert and, without their supervision, no work was to be done. So, with his usual howling, Gruber only said that if he'd catch anyone near the open wagons, he'd shoot them for plundering.

Because the death sentence seemed too much for a handful of sugar, at least for as long as we had some supply left, we did not go near those wagons for a few days, but after a regular bombing a new wagon was hit and both its sides were left open. The smell of half-burnt sugar got to be too much for us, because we had no more sugar left. One of our friends our age, whom we called 'Foxie' because of his audacity, wanted to go and renew our supply, but Tibi was against it because he said that if Gruber saw us we wouldn't need sugar any more. We were able to stand it for two days, but not more. The third day, when we saw that Gruber was going away, Foxie and I decided to try our luck and furtively went to the wagon, climbed up and began to fill our pockets.

THE TUMBLER

'Halt!' roared Gruber and, without waiting a moment longer, shot the poor Foxie in the forehead.

He must have been a sharpshooter. I remember thinking that it is interesting that when you get hit in the forehead, you don't fall backwards, but on your face. Not that I had much time to think about it because Gruber, without waiting a second, turned his handgun against me and for a fraction of a second I looked right into its barrel. I then did a flip-flop backwards, a thing I was unable to do before nor would do afterwards, and fell on my feet. I heard the bullet whiz by my ear, but somehow escaped by crawling under the wagons to get back to Tibi, who had heard the shots and was sure that I was gone. One interesting thing I should mention: for that millisecond that I looked into the barrel of the handgun, the hole seemed as big as a football, even bigger in my dreams, and that millisecond seemed to last hours. This dream, that recurred often, was not one of my favourite ones.

In the evening, when we returned to the camp, Gruber stood by the gate and I think that he searched for me, but I exchanged my knitted cap with the ear warmer for a regular blue and white one, rolled up my long coat and he did not recognise me. Of course, if he had searched my pockets he would have found the white, unburned sugar, but he did not. When Tibi saw the sugar, he wanted to kill me for not throwing it away. Throw it away? I didn't even think about it. This turned out to be a sweet evening: even the coffee we filled half full with sugar because Tibi did not want any to remain in case of a search. The next morning, we saw that the young guards were all gone. It seemed that they had been taken to the front and only the oldies remained. Were they all like Gruber? The truth is that I don't remember.

22 March 1945. I am sure that there is not one of Hildesheim's residents of my age, or around it, who doesn't remember that date with a shudder. The daily alarm sounded. It was a warm, splendid spring day, cloudless and clear, that filled one's heart with happiness. The smell of wet earth, the beginning and promise of the summer's blooming, the crystal-clear air, the blue skies, it all that made you breathe in the balmy air with joy. We lay on our

backs and looked up at the clear skies. The aeroplanes seemed somehow nearer than usual, and against the blue background their silvery images were like small fish swimming in a big aquarium. The armada that consisted of more than three hundred heavy bombers did not continue to Hanover as usual. They flew in a huge circle around the hill with the cemetery and over the city. When the planes closed the circle over the town, one of them flew into the middle of the circle, just over our nose and it shot a red rocket. At that sign all three hundred planes released all their bombs on the city below them, all together. That is the so-called carpet-bombing: very impressive. For some seconds there was silence, then a deep, terrible crash and the earth itself trembled. The blue skies and the daylight disappeared and were covered by thick, black, oily smelling smoke. Instead of the fresh smell of the wet earth, your nose was attacked by the unforgettable sulphuric stench of the disintegrating city. The daylight became a black night into which red tongues of burning gas and fuel rose. It was a terrible, frightening, but also majestic, vision. The work, dreams, hopes, art, property of centuries were burned and annihilated in a few moments or hours of man's madness.

As I sat there, not wanting to believe what I witnessed, I saw another picture in my imagination. Seven years before, in the last days of the late Czechoslovakian Republic, after Hitler's threats, there were anti-aircraft defence exercises in Kassa too. As I explained earlier, Father brought home a short cardboard pipe, painted red for its role as a bomb. We filled a pail with water and put a hand-pump with a two-metre long garden hose into it. Mother pumped with energy and I pointed the hose heroically at the bomb that succumbed at once, and we enjoyed the well-earned applause of the neighbours. The picture I saw in my mind was that of my mother and I putting out the burning hell that was once, only half an hour ago, the city of Hildesheim with a bucket of water and a two-metre long garden-hose. I was suddenly overcome by a fit of hysterical laughter that I was unable to stop. 'Shut up, you idiot,' hissed Tibi, 'because of you they will kill all of us on the spot.' I knew that, but was unable to stop. Tibi and the rest did the only possible thing: they laid me on my belly and sat on me until the fit passed. At last Tibi said, 'If you really want to laugh, think about where we will sleep, and what we will eat in the evening.' I thought about it and did not think it very funny. The official statistics stated that, in that half an hour, seventy percent of the city was destroyed, twenty-four days before the end of the war. Seventy percent? I did not see the thirty percent that remained.

The bombing had been over for more than two hours, but we did not move. We sat there in the cemetery because the guards did not know what to do. Under us the city was aflame and the oily, choking smoke crept higher and higher up the hill. Gruber decided that we would descend, but not toward the station where we came from as that was now a sea of flames, but on the other side. The way through the burning city was not easy because the smoking ruins closed the roads, and here and there chunks of mortar fell off the unsafe walls. The big gas-tank was still burning and we wandered about not knowing where to go. I knew that those people who were now running, dazzled and without knowing where to, were the same ones who had voted for Hitler and had cried 'hurray' with enthusiasm when the Nazis themselves did the same to the whole of Europe. But, in spite of myself, I was sorry for that centuries-old town. It had taken only one idiot, who had the right rank for it, to decide a few weeks before the end of war, while smoking his pipe, to destroy it without any aim or purpose. It would have been sufficient just to bomb a bridge or some rails, and then, our war too would have ended, as we hoped with their repair. Then I looked at Gruber who was busy beating one of the unfortunates, and all my merciful thoughts about the city and its citizens evaporated. Let them all perish.

After some more dithering about, we went in the same direction as a large group of people that comprised mostly women with baby carriages and blankets. Our goal was the small lake just outside the city. There the smoke was less thick and smelly and here and there you were even able to see the sky. It was already quite late and you could feel the chilly evening air. We blessed the fact that we had brought both our coats and blankets with us. There were some who were without. 'Luckily, there is no rain,' I told Tibi, and felt the first drops. Food we could only dream about. The sergeant sent someone to the camp, that is to the Variety building, but he came back without even finding the street. Luckily he found a bombed bakery, stole a baby carriage and filled it with bread, for the soldiers, naturally. When the women saw that Gruber wanted the bread for the soldiers only, they ran to him and in the melee one of ours stole two loaves of bread. While he was running away, one loaf fell down near us. Tibi caught it and hid it and that was the only bread we saw for some days.

It was not an easy night. We had to sleep with one eye open to stop our blankets from being stolen. The morning after, the first signs of the organising talent of the Germans were evident: they moved the women and children up to the unharmed church on the hill. They brought warm coffee and bread for the guards, and, because Gruber was absent, his second in command decided that we too should get a cup of coffee. But bread? Forget it, that was for the guards only.

Gruber came back in the afternoon but without any food to the great disappointment of the soldiers. Without any counting we got on our way. Our destination was, or so the rumours said, a camp some twenty kilometres after Hanover. It meant, I thought, at least three days of marching without food, because it was not likely that we would get anything. Our only hope was that perhaps we'd be able to 'organise' something by the wayside.

When we came to the highway, we saw that we were not the only ones. It was full of people who were running away before the approaching British and Americans. Unlike the situation in the East where all were fleeing before the Russians, there was two-way traffic as some were going in the direction of the cities, which were already in the hands of the Allied armies. I concluded that the population was weary of the war and knew that the collapse of the regime was near. Not that it helped us. In the meantime the roads, that were full of people, only showed that it wouldn't be easy to find something to eat by the wayside, or a place to sleep. That was exactly what happened and the second night we slept with empty stomachs. There were some, mainly among those marching towards the front, who tried to throw us something to eat, but Gruber fulfilled his role heroically, and explained that we were only dirty Jews. He was very surprised that there were some people on whom that made no impression now.

On the third night after the bombing we came to the outskirts of Hanover. Before the war this city was one of the biggest and most important cities in Germany, with more than half a million people, multi-storeyed houses on both sides of the wide streets and thoroughfares. So it was once. Now, after the unceasing bombings for months and months, there was not a single house with more than one storey. The ruins of the higher storeys had fallen onto the streets and made them impassable, with the exception of a narrow strip, barely enough for a truck to pass. This strip was widened every two hundred metres for the cars that came from the other direction, where they had to wait to let the traffic pass. Between these bypasses there was one-way traffic only.

In these heaps of ruins there would occasionally be a wobbling, lonely wall or half a room that a bomb left untouched, and you could see a tablecloth fluttering in the wind, with the remains of a half-eaten meal, or a bedroom showing the half-made beds without shame to the whole world. Hanover looked like a city where only ghosts dwelled, but there were many people living there in cellars and holes. It could be seen even from the many gallows that stood on every other corner. These gallows were nothing like what you see in movies, nothing elaborate like that. These were true German utility gallows, for mass-consumption. They looked like a coat hanger, some two and half metres wide and not higher than that; on every one of them five or six people hung on a very short noose. Most of them were foreign 'volunteer' workers and on their bodies there was a placard that proclaimed 'Plundering means death'. These pictures accompanied us over many kilometres: pictures of Europe and the German civilisation in the middle of the twentieth century. The guards, and Gruber, of course, made us nearly run through the city so that the daily visit of the bombers would not catch us there.

We reached the outskirts of the city completely exhausted. Here the road was empty and Gruber, who in Hanover did not want people to witness it, felt free now to shoot down two men and seemed very pleased. Most of the guards did not like it but nobody said a word. Tibi and I walked together and helped each other, but did not talk because we had no strength left. I think that we did not walk more than a few kilometres, but I am not sure, because everything was unclear and we lifted our feet like automatons. At last we got to the camp and fell down, half dead, on the floor.

It was an extraordinary camp, as Nazi camps go. When we opened our eyes, we got a third of bread, a spoon of marmalade and hot coffee. There were people who wept from happiness. In Hebrew hunger is called 'raav' and those who suffer from hunger are said to be suffering from 'harpat raav', 'the shame of hunger'. You are ashamed in your own eyes that you, like an animal, are unable to control your hunger, and he who sees you in your shame – if he is a man worthy of that name – is ashamed that he has to see you like that. But, let's leave the philosophy.

As I said, this was an extraordinary camp. There were not more than two hundred and fifty prisoners, nearly all Germans, many of whom had been prisoners for more than ten years, from the first days of the Nazi regime. They too wore the blue and white pyjamas, but on them they looked better and you saw that they were changed from time to time. Over the jacket pocket on a white strip was their number and an upwards-pointing triangle that showed their 'crime': red for the political, communist and social democrat prisoners, green for the criminals, lilac for the homosexuals and black for the priests. If the man was a Jew too, on the upward pointing triangle there was a yellow, downward

175

THE TUMBLER

pointing triangle, and so the two triangles formed the Star of David. There were not many of the latter and they were mainly among the political prisoners, but I saw a priest like that too. After the long years in the camps, they did not look their best but, compared to us, they were prizefighters of course. Their guards were wounded SS, convalescing after the hospital. The prisoners knew their rights and it seemed the soldiers respected them. They spoke to our 'Volkssturm' guard with a cold disdain that we enjoyed very much.

The old prisoners' feelings toward us were a mixture of pity, disgust and fear. With their brain they knew that our disgusting appearance was due to mistreatment and hunger and that we were being driven from place to place without the possibility of washing or changing our clothes. But, emotionally, they despised us for it and, chiefly, they were afraid because they were sure that the Germans would kill us, and they did not want to be around when that happened because such things can be contagious. Who can blame them? In addition, we were twice their number and they did not get food for us. Both the SS and the prisoners themselves did everything in their power so that we should leave as soon as possible.

This camp had worked for nearly two years drilling and digging tunnels into the mountain for the V3 rockets that in those days started to attack London, and that was Hitler's hope for victory. They had already drilled more than three kilometres into the mountain and the completion of the project was scheduled for July, but everybody knew that the war would be over before that. The prisoners worked in two twelve-hour shifts, and they knew that when the work was completed the Germans would kill them, so they tried to work slowly. That was another reason why they wanted us to move on as soon as possible.

The work itself consisted of drilling holes into the rock with two metre long steel drills, stuffing the holes with dynamite, blowing them up and taking away the debris in carts. It was clear that they did not want us to rest. They wanted to put me with the drillers. The work was done in such a way that the drill was laid on an upward slanting board and you had to push it to do its work. It was soon clear that for this work I'd have to weigh at last thirty kilograms more, so they transferred me to concreting.

Here, the world got richer with a patent, for which I should get the Nobel Prize someday, if there is any justice. Let's describe it for the benefit of future generations. The cement for the concrete and the mortar came in sacks that had three layers: the outer one, which was torn and dirty, the inner one with cement on it, and the middle one that was clean. The tearing of the sacks was forbidden of course, like everything else, but you could get away with it, and I saw that the old and pampered ones tore up the middle sack for toilet paper. It was cold in the tunnels so I tore out a whole middle sack. I cut out a hole for my head, two on the sides for the arms, cut it in the front and wore it under my shirt. Because the paper had insulating qualities I felt much warmer and better. You now think, of course, that the insulation was the patent. You are wrong. At the end of the shift I had to take it off so that the guards would not see it. The sack almost began to walk by itself. It seems that the lice, their parents, grandparents and future generations, all wandered over to the sack, and that is why I felt much better. I must admit that, in spite of the mass-emigration, they did leave enough eggs to ensure the life of the future generations. I leave this patent for the benefit of the grateful posterity, but I keep all the rights as the discoverer. We worked there for five nights and at the end I felt very much better because of the temporary absence of the lice.

During the last days, the food got much worse as we received only a quarter of bread without anything on it; the soup got much thinner too and we did not get the same as the old prisoners. One morning at ten they tore us out of the beds (let's not forget, that we worked till eight o'clock on the night-shift) and we were on our way again. Our guards began to feel their age, and even Gruber shut up for a change. He stumbled along with the last ones and we were only sorry that there was no one to shoot him.

I don't think that we walked more than ten kilometres on the first day and, after a cold, rainy night, we got up with an empty belly again. The guards had something left from what they got or stole for the way, but they knew that even for them there wouldn't be much more until we reached our destination, so they beat us to go faster. At the next village two wounded SS joined us, and from then on the sound of them shooting the last prisoners was what made us pick up our feet. It seemed that other camps had walked here before us because, as we went, we often saw pyjama-clad bloody skeletons in the ditches. These roads too were full of fleeing Germans who were not sure where they wanted to go and it was interesting to hear their opinion now about what they saw. When before all we heard was 'Saujude', now many of them spat when they saw how we looked and how we were treated, and murmured that it was a shame and that they would have to suffer soon because of what these hangmen did. It is hard to believe how human the Germans get before a defeat.

I don't know if it took another day or two before we got to the open railway wagons which, after one day only, took us to our destination. What I do know is that during all this time we did not eat anything, and the hunger ate us. From our wagon only we had to throw out three more dead. At last we stopped. I knew the place. I remembered the stench. After two months, we were back at the station of Bergen-Belsen.

We were hardly able to drag ourselves along the short way to the gate of the camp. The guards of the Volkssturm were in not much better shape, in spite of the fact that most of them had been able to buy some bread in the last village. There were twice as many as at our last visit who made the last metres to the gate on all fours, but they shot only those who did not move so that they would not have too many cadavers to carry. Even so, there were some fifteen bodies, not that anybody counted. At the gate they sent our guards home, at their great relief. It seemed that they wanted to spare their sensitive souls from seeing the best of German creativity: Bergen-Belsen, 3 April 1945.

If at our previous visit I described this place as hell, now it was the lowest ring of hell under the management of devils of German origin. The 'Appelplatz', which last time was empty and clean, was now full of living and dead skeletons. The living ones stopped from time to time to relieve themselves. Among them there were some who were even able to lower their pants beforehand, and some who were even able to get up afterwards. Typhus and hunger made people fill their bellies with water, when there was water, with nearly instant result: what went in through the mouth, went out through the other end. The barracks were not full but they were not empty either: there were dead men and dying ones and those who had no strength or will to get up to relieve themselves. I went to our capo, Pinter, and said that he should organise an empty barrack for us, but he was wholly apathetic and unable to do anything. Eventually, Tibi and I, together with some boys with whom it was still possible to talk, took out the dead men, lay the dying together and cleaned a corner for ourselves. We threw out the straw and brought in some half clean blankets – there were enough to go around - for sleeping. The old inmates told us that they had not had bread for more than a week, and for two days not even the usual soup.

The next morning we saw some Italian and British prisoners of war digging a pit. It was some fifty by fifty meters wide and more than two meters deep. They had an SS guard, not to guard them but so that the Jews would not go there begging for food. Other than that, there were not even patrols by day and you could see guards only on the watchtowers. We went to sleep hungry and I could not remember the last time we had eaten.

The next day, it must have been the seventh or eighth of April, a capo came and asked who was ready for some work, for a soup. Of course, we agreed. He led us to a closed barrack and opened the door. And now, please believe me, because I know that it sounds incredible, and I know why it sounds incredible, but I don't want to go into the disgusting details more than I must, but I have to tell the truth as it was.

As I said, he opened the door and we felt the stench. As I remember it, it was not much worse than the stench outside. The barrack was full of naked cadavers, ten in a row, crosswise: where the first row's feet were, the second row's heads were. There were some ten rows in each heap, stacked like firewood, and there were five such heaps. That is, some hundreds of 'things' that were once people like you and I.

The reason for this mode of storing bodies was that some months before, in the freezing days of winter, it was not yet acceptable to let the bodies lay about everywhere. The courtyard of the small crematorium was full and it was difficult to dig the frozen earth. They thought that when it got warmer, they would bury them. Then, it became clear that the British would be there in a few days, and the sensitive souls of the Germans did not want to leave such a picture for the enemy as they could get the wrong impression, God forbid.

Before I go into detail and in an answer to your question how these bodies, laying on each other, could remain relatively whole, you must not think about them as bodies, but as mummies, consisting of dried out skins and bones. You see, the old Egyptians had a whole complicated process of making mummies out of dead people but the Germans, with their technology and progress, made mummies out of bodies when they were technically still alive.

But let's return to our subject: our role was to empty the barrack and take the bodies to the big pit that the prisoners of war had been digging, some two hundred meters away. It was out of the question to take them on a stretcher: there was no time for that, no stretchers, no strength. We tied a rope to the arms or feet of the bodies and dragged them to the pit. I took my half-torn belt from my trousers, which I tied up with a rope, and the body I tied with my belt. Tibi looked at me and asked why I was doing that, and I explained that the rope I would throw away, but the belt I'd keep as a 'keepsake', because without it I would not be able to believe what I did, where and why. He said that I was completely out of my mind and he was probably right, but the belt I still have with me and I still need to look at it in order to believe what I did.

We formed a line of two men dragging a body. At the head there were two tall men, who even then looked more like men than skeletons and whom we called the giraffes, who dragged a body each, and after them the rest. This picture is deeply engraved in my mind, even if it is hard to believe that I had a mind where my brain used to be: the grey, cloudy sky; the living skeletons dragging the dead ones at a snail's pace when, from time to time, one of the dragging ones became a dragged one, but not before taking off his clothes, because the Germans wouldn't let us bury something that could be of some use.

It was time for lunch and from afar we saw the vat-bearers. I ran and was among the first ones. I was afraid that the cook would give me a thin soup from the top, but he did it as it should be done and gave me the thick soup from the bottom. Tibi finished the hot soup in two gulps, ran back to get another helping and came back shouting why I didn't go and get another bowl of soup. He found me nearly weeping. 'I don't eat beetroot,' I sobbed. 'What do you mean, you don't eat beetroot?' he shouted, wanting to throttle me. 'You eat every kind of garbage, like we all do, don't you?'

He was right of course. Half rotten potatoes? No problem. Potato peels from the garbage heap? I can't have enough of them. Cattle turnips, I don't ask from where. If I would say a blessing for food, I would say it twice with enthusiasm for them. But beetroots, I am truly sorry, I do not eat, period.

'You imbecile, we have not seen food for more than a week, and who knows when we will get something again and you behave like a spoilt child in Bergen-Belsen?!' growled Tibi.

I wept and forced myself to swallow a mouthful, but was unable to do it. At last, when Tibi saw that I couldn't eat it, he gave me his empty soup, and I gave him the beetroots. In the meantime, the other skeletons too saw that there was some food and they drove away the cooks, ran to the vats, turned them over and tried to lick up the soup from the earth. Shame! The shame of hunger.

After half an hour I was full of remorse and cursed myself for not being able to force it down. I can't do it today either.

After lunch we went back to our disgusting job. Tibi and I specialised on the draggers who fell dead in the middle of the way, and on the parts of bodies that were left on the floor. Let's not get into the subject of why: they were lighter than the whole bodies and they were nearer to the pit. In addition, we did not have to get into the barrack, which became more and more disgusting the nearer we got to the bodies at the bottom of the piles. We continued the next day too and, as lunchtime got nearer, I told Tibi that no matter what would be in the soup he should stuff it in my mouth, by force if necessary. But there was no such a problem because, in spite of the promises, we got nothing. We did not get anything the next day either.

The third day, and from here the days get more and more blurred, was full of sleeping and waking up with a start to relieve myself, of hunger and an impotent weakness. Did I think about death? No, I did not, and I don't know why. I only remember that the capo came and told us that he saw an SS man slip away in civilian clothes. The capo was not in too bad a condition and it seemed that he had had something to eat in the morning, but now he suddenly wanted to build better relations with the rank and file. There was a change in the air. The only question was what would arrive first: the change or the angel of death? Did I say the angel of death? There is no doubt, that no heavenly messenger would come to Bergen-Belsen, only some devil from the hell, who got nominated as his deputy, and covered his face in shame, at how much better the Germans fulfil his shameful assignment.

The next day, people came and said that there was a white flag on the watchtower near the gate. After some people demolished the fences, I too went to the former food store. As the legend tells it, the first one found some bread there but I did not see any. What did I see? Beetroots!! If it had not been for the cattle turnip I found not far away, I am sure that I would have gone and hanged myself. I ate the turnip, and the beetroots I took to Tibi. We went into the barrack and, because we had something in our bellies, we slept till the next morning.

The next day was a real spring day and the sun shone. I went out, found a clean place for us to sit, and went back to take Tibi with me. To my horror, he did not show any will to move and in his eyes I saw the first signs of hopeless resignation. Eventually, I dragged him out. We slept in the sun and at ten o'clock a great noise woke us up. It was a British tank demolishing the gate and all the other fences too.

Somebody in the tank announced through a loudspeaker, 'We are the Army of His Majesty, the King of Great Britain, and we have come to free you. You are free!' and he repeated it again and again, in English, German, Yiddish, Hungarian, Russian and Rumanian, and from his accent you heard that he had it written down for him. 'You are free, you are free!'

I fearfully approached the officer and asked him in English, 'What day is today?'

He looked at me as if he could not believe his eyes and answered with shock, mixed with pity and revulsion, 'Today is the fifteenth of April, 1945.' It was two days before my seventeenth birthday.

17

The Liberation

The tank trundled around the camp twice, and the cheering and shouts of joy followed it. I wrote down this sentence and stopped to reconsider. *Cheering? Joy? Shouts?* It was something more like the whimpering of half dead skeletons. We had waited, wanted and prayed for the liberation every day and every moment of every day. What remains now, to wait for, to pray for? A kind of tired, grey, hopeless weariness was in the air.

In the two months following the liberation, more than twenty thousand people died in Bergen-Belsen. They say that it was because of the fatty food, which was too heavy for the dried out stomachs of the skeletons that had long forgotten what food was; and it is true.

It is also true that typhus, cholera and the devil knows what other illnesses continued to take their toll. They say that in the military hospitals they had no experience of caring for the victims of systematic starving and torture. All that is true but, in my opinion, it is not less true that now, after the long awaited liberation, many in the camps thought that there was nothing more to wait for; and that was, alas, true for many, many people.

The British opened some field-kitchens so that we did not have to go too far for food, but Tibi had not the strength or will to go even that far, so I took his mess tin too. There was a fat soup from conserves, potatoes and one third of bread. I could not take that and the soup too, and did not have the strength to go back a second time, so I only took the bread and potatoes. I was very lucky because the fat soup renewed the diarrhea and it caused the death of many. We ate the bread and the potatoes and they helped to ease the hunger, which burned like a fire in our bellies. It would take a long time before we were able to feel satiety.

After eating, I felt stronger and decided to go and visit the nearby camp of women. Afterwards, I wished I had not done it. Looking at it objectively, it was not worse than our camp: there too were heaps of naked skeletons outside, the same stench inside the barracks, the only difference being that they had two-storied plank beds. Here too, there were many who were not able to get out to relieve themselves and here too, there were dead and dying skeletons inside. There were some who quarrelled in screeching voices and vehemently gesticulated with their skeleton arms. Surprisingly, there were some who looked better, and they stood one after the other waiting for a mirror, to comb their hair. 'Das ewig weibliche' - the eternal woman. I had wanted to ask if there was anybody from Kassa, but I did not dare because I was afraid that I would find someone I knew looking like that, and fled back to where I had come from.

These images haunt me to this very day and with them the impotent rage against those who did that to our girls and women, the shame for the women and the bigger shame for myself because of the instinctive disgust that accompanied the endless pity and compassion. Is it a later rationalisation now for my feelings then? No, I don't think so. There are many memories that have long since faded, but not that one, nor the feeling of rage and horror at seeing the women there. I understood the instinctive recoiling and disgust in the eyes of that English officer, whom I asked what day it was, or in those who see the motion pictures of those camps, or perhaps even in those who read these lines now.

After the liberation came the reporters and the photographers, whose reports told about the Hungarian, Polish, Slovakian and Russian prisoners. That was, of course, no more than a previously agreed fiction. Ninety-five percent of us were Jews, who were dragged to gas chambers, to mass graves, to Bergen-Belsen simply because we were Jews and for that reason only, no matter in which country we were born. We lay in the sun and heard the rumours.

Azriel Feuerstein

They said that the British had captured a lot of fleeing SS and, in their first rage after seeing the situations in the camps, they loaded them on a truck and, driving from lamppost to lamppost, they made the SS hang each other. It was of course no more than a beautiful dream. The lawsuit of some of them took years and, at the end, their sentence was a mockery of justice. Some of them fled the country or lived in Germany under an assumed name, and only very few of them were hanged, among whom Kremer, the commandant of Bergen-Belsen and Höss, the commandant of Auschwitz. But even that was better than nothing.

Now we, in Bergen-Belsen, had to be satisfied with less: the captured SS men and women had to take the dead bodies on stretchers to the mass graves. We saw with great satisfaction how they, who only yesterday were the lords of life and death, humbled themselves now before every British private. One half-dead skeleton, not far away from me, and whom an SS woman thought to be dead, took a fistful of excrement and threw it in her face. The Tommy who guarded her turned a blind eye. I thought to myself that she deserved a bigger portion, but she raised her hand threateningly until the soldier's rifle butt reminded her that this is a new order and drove her back to work. Tibi was very apathetic the whole time and hardly answered when I spoke to him, but I did not desist because there is nothing easier and more dangerous than to glide from such a temporary apathy into lasting death.

After some hours Tibi recovered a little. The British brought groups of Germans to the camp from the neighbouring towns: well dressed men and women who had to pass by the pits which contained thousands of bodies and the skeletons still lying about, and were made to get inside the stinking barracks. The women covered their delicate noses with lace handkerchiefs and turned away in disgust from those who were unable to restrain themselves and had to relieve themselves then and there. The civilians had to see and smell all this, like a dog that gets his nose pushed in his own excrement to teach him that certain things are not done. They all swore that they did not know what was going on in the camp. I believe that when they got home, they succeeded in convincing themselves that these Jewish skeletons, who were not ashamed even to excrete in public, had nothing in common with civilised people like themselves and probably deserved their lot. These groups continued to arrive only for a few days, because they had convinced a high ranking British officer that these visits would cause a traumatic reaction in women. After that they brought only Nazi functionaries but, after a week, these visits too ceased.

In the meantime, Tibi was overcome by a dangerously tiring weakness. He did not care about anything and it seems that it infected me too, because I don't remember the next few days at all.

After a week we were told that they'd transfer us to the former SS barracks. Before that, we had to undergo a procedure that half of Europe also went through at that time: the hair from all over the body was shaved off and a liberal doze of DDT against lice powdered us. We were also washed all over: that is, they tried to remove the uppermost layer of the dirt that in the last month had become an integral part of our skin. The whole thing was done, under the supervision of a British soldier, by two Hungarian soldiers, prisoners of war who came with the Germans of their own free will. They did their work as it should be done but with obvious disgust at my glee. 'They made you a servant of the Jews?' I asked one with irony, and he looked at me with hate in his eyes.

Here, for the second time, I felt the fear of death. The first time was in Bergen-Belsen, at the sight of the man with the pushcart who whacked the dying man over the head. The second time was now, when I became aware of my impotence and weakness, and that my life was now nothing more than a small spark that could be blown out without effort. I was afraid that this Hungarian soldier would find the opportunity to do it. Luckily, the British soldier was with us all the way and accompanied us to the barracks of the SS. Here, Tibi and I were separated because they took him straight to the hospital. That was the last time I saw

Tibi, who had been a friend and a brother to me in times when there were no friends and no brothers.

The SS quarter was a row of two storey houses. In a spacious room there were three double beds, a washbasin, a mirror, a wardrobe and a door to the lavatory. The beds were made with white sheets and covers. I chose an upper bed and was sure that I had come to heaven before my time. To heaven I did not arrive but it seemed that I was not far away because I was unable to eat anything but bread, and did not even go down to eat. I don't remember much of those days. During that time, some of my roommates in better condition tried to find some relatives or friends on the lists that began to arrive at the central office and there were even some who tried to visit them. I, for my part, heard that there was an infirmary on the other side of the road and decided that I'd go there the following day. So the next day I got up and was on my way for the great journey.

There is much that I have forgotten, but this undertaking I remember in detail. I descended the steps, holding the banister all the way, and sat down at the curb. The 'Autobahn', a fifty metre wide highway like those others that Hitler had built for his thankful people, stretched before me like a great ocean, with the infirmary on the other side, and I had to plan how to navigate this distance. I was on the verge of postponing this adventure for the day, but didn't because I did not feel up to climbing those steps again. At last, I found the willpower and arrived at the infirmary.

There, an English doctor asked me my name and age in German. When I said that I was seventeen years old, behind my back he made a sign on his forehead, signalling to the nurse that I was crazy and said to her in English, 'Write down forty.' Only after I told him in broken English the exact date of my birth and the first four lines of the poem 'The Raven', could I convince him that I knew what I was talking about. After a careful examination he took my temperature, which was less than 38 degrees. He said to me that he believed I'd get typhus, but it was not certain. That is why he did not send me to the hospital, but said that if I felt worse, I should go straight there. He gave me some aspirins, two of which I took there and then, and weighed me. I weighed twenty-five kilos. A year before I had weighed forty kilos more and my dream had been to lose as much weight as possible. That is the way dreams look when they are made true by devils.

I crossed the highway, got back to my room, and felt that the aspirin was beginning to help. The next day, I got my appetite back and was able to eat the soup. I was able to get to the office where I left my particulars for those who were looking for me and for those I wanted to find. It is interesting to remark that, in the camps, we used to speak about finding our families but now, for some reason, I was sure that they were no more. For a few days I felt better and went to the office to ask if anybody knew where Tibi was, but nobody knew about him. In the evening I remembered the obvious: to go to the hospital and ask there. I resolved to do it the next morning.

That evening, the sister of a Polish roommate from a nearby camp came to visit her brother. This girl had the incredible luck of belonging to a group that was sent some months before the end of the war to a small village to work in the fields because all their men had been called up. The women there were grateful for the help and the girls ate at the same table with the families and got the same food. You could see it on her because, far from being a skeleton, she was a bit plump, and the menu of their dinners we heard as stories from the fables. As the bed under me was empty, she lied down there to sleep.

Next morning I woke up feeling bad. I opened my eyes and looked down. The girl was lying there naked as on the day she was born, but much more adorned with all the attributions, that are so dear for the eyes, and stimulates other parts. But – nothing was stimulated, nothing moved, not even after some gentle prodding. *Well*, I said to myself, *that is it*. Mourning the untimely demise of my youth, I got down from my bed, covered the girl and started to the hospital, feeling worse with every step.

When I arrived there, I sat down and it seems that I swooned. I awoke when a nurse took my temperature. It was over forty degrees. I wanted to ask about Tibi, but lost consciousness before

I was able to. I awoke feeling a fresh smelling female hand stroking my brow, and heard the nurse saying to the doctor:

'It seems that the boy is with us again.'

'We'll send him to Sweden to recover a bit', answered the doctor in German and he turned to me.

'Do you want to go to Sweden, Yuray?' he asked, and I nodded weakly in agreement with half closed eyes.

Sweden... snow... North ... Scandinavia... peace ... food ... Selma Lagerlöf...

I felt relaxed, I felt that the temperature was going down and I slowly fell into a half slumber. GYURIKA!!!

18

Fröken Ulle

I did not see Fröken Ulle for three days. I thought that perhaps she must have had a lot of work to do. Some of the students were back already and I was sure that the five o'clock tea would be served in the little dining room. There was no need to pamper Yeory with special room service any more. Never mind. I thought we'd meet there and that I'd have the opportunity to thank her for her kindness during the holidays. Until then, I sat down to finish some lessons, which I had left for the last day, a thing I didn't usually do. I was closing the copybooks when somebody knocked.

As my eyes caught sight of her I almost shouted with joy, 'Hey, Fröken Ulle, I thought that you had so much work that you had forgotten me.'

'How can you say that? It was you who left without telling me!' replied Fröken Ulle in a hurt tone.

'Not so, Fröken Ulle, I left you a note in the office telling you that I was going to Gothenburg and, as luck would have it, I had to sleep over.'

'Ya-so, that is the lady's name, Luck? But it is true that in the last few days I have had no opportunity to go to the office and look in my drawer,' explained Fröken Ulle.

I defensively replied, 'You see, Fröken Ulle, you are accusing innocents. I see that you have brought my copybook. Have you finished the long chronicle of my short life? What did you think of it?'

Fröken Ulle laid down the implements of her trade, the yellow dust cloth and the feather duster, always a sign that she had something of importance to say, and put the copybook on the table.

'I thought about how lucky people like you are, who survived all this and now have something to talk about all their life.'

'You have no idea how right you are.'

Epilogue

The Tumbler

1947. Two years after the liberation of Bergen-Belsen. We don't talk much about what happened. It is finished. The dreams don't occur as often as before. I have finished the course in Folkhögskolan Fjaelhoegen and, because I had now learned Swedish and had a certificate too, I got a job in an office, which gave me great prestige in our circles, but very low wages. So, I gave up my elevated social position, moved from the village to Gothenburg and got a position as a simple worker but for twice as much pay, and also enrolled to study at university in the evening.

In Gothenburg there were many survivors like me and there were vigorous Zionist activities with a weekly meeting every Saturday night. On such an evening I met my future sister-in law, Olga, and through her, her sister and my future wife, Annie. The two had, an apartment in a very old house, but in the very middle of the city, and it became a social centre. Olga was an accomplished and well-known seamstress, as she was successful in everything she did.

Within a short time I felt myself very much at home with them. Nearly every day after work, I came up to them for a chat, coffee and to meet with the boys who came there to meet with the girls. There was a strong connection and a deep love between Olga and Annie. They were the oldest of eight sisters and brothers, and the only survivors of their big and deeply religious family. Olga was the oldest, the leader, the one who made the decisions. They were both very beautiful, each one in her own way. Olga was instantly conspicuous in every society with her typical Jewish beauty, her sparkling black hair, vivacious nature and humorous temperament. Annie's beauty was more classic, still and reserved.

Soon, we began to go out, but it was not simple. Then, as now, Annie preferred to sit at home. I said, 'sit?' The truth is that then, as now, you could seldom find her sitting. She was always busy cooking, cleaning and mending and, in order to convince her to come with us, Olga and I had to make a sacred promise that we were only going for a walk and window-shopping. In the course of the walk, we 'accidentally' came to a cinema, and Annie had no other choice but to come in with us. Of course, she did not let us forget that all this was against her will. At the end she enjoyed the show and with time and much effort and luck, I convinced her to enjoy other diversions too.

I loved Sweden very much from the first moment on. In those years following the Second World War, when the whole of Europe was in ruins, Sweden was an island of tranquillity, peace and cleanliness. I was impressed by the honesty of its people. Nearly everywhere you could leave your door open without fear of being robbed. In a village it was a common sight in the mornings to see people on their way to work leaving sums of money with the paperwork on the counter of the post office, which opened later, to find the receipt in the evening when they returned from work.

I read the newspapers, took part in the cultural life, knew and liked the literature and the poetry, and through a Swedish girlfriend had access to the local intellectual circles. I had Swedish friends from the night school and from work but, in spite of all that, I didn't consider, even for a single moment, to remain there or to use the American affidavit my aunt sent me as soon as she heard that I had survived. I decided that, after finishing university, I was going to Palestine.

The situation in Palestine in 1947 was going from bad to worse. The Jews had to fight not only the Arabs, but also the English Mandate, which closed the doors to Jewish immigration at a time when the few Holocaust survivors were desperately trying to make Aliya (the Hebrew word for immigration to the Land of Israel). In Europe, the Jews returning to their former homes were met with an even stronger hatred than before, because their former neighbours were afraid that they would have to return the property they had stolen. These tortured people knew that they could not and would not stay in Europe and clamoured for the ceasing of the restrictions on emigration to Palestine.

Both Annie and I knew that we wanted to go to Palestine and we also knew that we wanted to stay together. We signed up as volunteers for the army, that is the Hagana, because there was no army and no state yet. Annie did not want me to leave the university and she was right since, because of the errors of those responsible for the Aliya from Sweden, we had to stay until December 1948. We finally got our departure date only two weeks beforehand.

We had no time for a civil marriage because you had to sign up four weeks before so, but thanks to the understanding of the rabbi, we got married in the synagogue, on 16 December, on my late mother's birthday. Because we had neither the time nor the money for a proper wedding, instead of an invitation we sent our friends a 'post factum notification' in both Hungarian and Swedish, and this is the way it read: 'We herewith announce our wedding/ No one got an invitation/ Forgive us, our dear friends, we hope/ you'll understand our situation/ only we two were there / and the rabbi of course and such / that is all that is important/ and it does not cost too much/ On a journey for a new Homeland/ we'll start with the help of Heaven/ Come up for a happy farewell/ every evening after seven.'

We added that we were going to Israel for our honeymoon and they awaited us with fireworks. The announcement was a big success, the marriage too, so far (touch wood), but who has ever heard of fireworks that last sixty years?

We said goodbye to friends and neighbours, to the peaceful life in Sweden, but the farewell that hurt most was to say goodbye to Olga, Annie's beloved sister. A short time after our departure she emigrated to America, where she met and married an old flame from home, Shol. They had three children. Some twenty years ago most of the family made Aliya and they are living not far from us. Even the second generation inherited our mutual love.

We left Gothenburg a week after the wedding, on 24 December 1948, Christmas Eve. I still see before me the city I came to love, covered with sparkling white snow and decorated with green branches of fir trees, as the festive illuminations were mirrored in the snow. In the evening we arrived into the dark, dirty and smelling Marseille, which now, three years after the end of the war, still bore its marks. Not for a moment did I regret my decision to leave Sweden, but I made up my mind there and then to renew contact with my Swedish friends, who would have the right to think me boorish and ungrateful. I wanted to separate the new and difficult life we had chosen from the old comfortable one. Here, in Marseille, as volunteers for the Army, we underwent a two-week military training with men and women in separate rooms, which is not an ideal condition for a honeymoon, but 'love finds a way.'

On 6 January 1949 we embarked on the 'Atzmaut' and, on the dawn of 11 January 1949, we arrived at Haifa, as the first rays of the sun touched Mount Carmel. Being on the upper deck, who were the first to see it, and began to sing the Hatikva at stiff attention, and after a few seconds the whole ship joined us, roaring. Since then I have never heard our national anthem sung so fervently and so out of tune.

Late afternoon we arrived at the former English military camp, now a camp for new immigrants in Pardess Hanna. Both of us were young, and so found a place for ourselves in a barrack while most of the others had to sleep in big military tents, which was not very nice in the rainy January weather. This barrack was a standard military one with brick walls and a tin roof. It was thirty metres long and eight metres wide, full of beds on both sides, half a metre away from each other. On every bed there was a straw mattress, a sheet and two covers. You can't say that these were ideal conditions for a honeymoon, but we only had our beds there.

The next evening my cousin, who lived in a nearby kibbutz, took us with him. There we got a small barrack for ourselves, which was not a small luxury. Its only drawback was that the Iraqi Army was only half a kilometre away and, occasionally, when they saw light in one of the barracks they tried to shoot somebody. It seems that we slept very well there because the first morning when we woke up, we found a bullet hole some half a meter above my bed. I remember that barrack with love. We stayed and worked in the kibbutz and only occasionally ventured to the camp in Pardess Hanna to ask for news about getting an apartment (there was no news about that) and to visit relatives from the camp, who were wise enough to emigrate before the Holocaust. The camp was near the highway.

In those times there were very few private cars, buses were very seldom – and they cost money - so if you had to go somewhere, you had to hitchhike. We had a scientific way of doing it: we had relatives in both directions, so Annie stood on the direction we preferred, and I on the other side. The philosophy behind it was that for whomever the car stopped, the second one hopped in. I am sorry to report that the cars always stopped on Annie's side. That much about Jewish solidarity!

With the help of my cousin Shmuel and his wife Pirha, we bought a one room and kitchen apartment, in one of the houses that grew out like mushrooms everywhere but were difficult to get.

Now that we had an apartment, I began to work on occasional jobs, as there were no other ones, in the building industry. It was not easy but we were young. Everybody around us was in the same situation and the air was full of cheerful optimism. My special luck was, then as now, my wife Annie.

There is a special kind of woman who, with a touch of their hands, are able to transform every place where they stay into a home. Annie is such a woman. Our two beds in the camp in Pardess Hanna were not the same as the others: a curtain divided them from the others and we had special bedspreads. The same happened in our barrack in the kibbutz and now in our one room apartment. As if by magic, curtains appeared on the windows, the two beds that every emigrant received from the Jewish Agency were transformed into an elegant sofa (OK, everything is relative!). The rough crate with the shelves became a bookcase, the table and the two simple chairs got covered with cushions, and the grey floor tiles became white in spite of themselves, from

THE TUMBLER

Annie's untiring and unceasing efforts. As soon as you opened the door, you saw that you had come home. No work is too much or too difficult for her and if she begins something, she must finish it, come hell or high water. About her she thinks, if at all, last. Her caring, grumbling love is the tie that binds our family together. The best, most beautiful present a child can get for his whole life is the knowledge that his parents love him and each other. Our children received that gift.

After many temporary and disappointing jobs, I got hired as a surveyor's helper, and later as a field surveyor, and for more than forty years I have been a self-employed surveyor with my own office. This profession gave me pride, satisfaction and a living. In every new village, chiefly in Galilee but elsewhere too, there are some drops of my sweat, as there are too in every new forest I planned and set out in the stony fields and hills before they were planted, and I don't forget to mention it when we drive by. My grandchildren kid me about it, but what do they know? They think that we got it all ready made.

As a surveyor I was often away from home. We were surveying and parceling the new villages, slept in a nearby kibbutz or hotel and I often came home only for the weekend. But Annie and I were happy because I had work and we had an apartment, something not everybody had at the time. Then, Annie got pregnant and she took it in her stride, like everything else, never complained and always found something to do.

We seldom spoke about the torments and sufferings we went through in the recent past, even between us. These things were too near and we were busy with work, the apartment, making a living and laying the foundations for our new life. We felt that we had to let the past take care of itself. In May 1950 my son, Yehuda, was born.

When I first held my newborn son in my arms, I was assaulted by confusing feelings. I was relieved that the birth was easy and that both Annie and the child were well. I felt elated and had a feeling of victory that, in spite of the fact that half the world had wanted to destroy us, we were here and had created a new life.

But at the same time, I felt a deep sorrow and bereavement that my parents could not see their grandchild and me, as a young father. I felt that I would be able to do anything to keep this child from everything bad and dangerous. I understood the feeling of my parents and many millions of other Jewish parents who, while they were enduring their own terrible fate, had to suffer the helplessness, the impotence, the shame of not being able to help those creatures whose fate was more important to them than their own life. For that, no forgiveness and no vengeance are possible.

Our son, Yehuda, was a beautiful baby. He grew, got stronger and with him our pride and joy – and our fear and worry grew too. We did not talk about it at first, but we were anxious about the child: did he not inherit the terrible memories of our past? When he awakes at night crying, is it not our nightmares that disturb him? Does he smile and laugh enough, like other babies his age? At first, I did not share these worries with Annie, but I saw that she too had the same fears.

The boy was already six months old, able to turn on his belly and rise on his elbows. He recognised me and welcomed me with a smile when I returned from work. Every new gesture increased our pleasure, but did not let us forget our worries. At the time I was new in the office, often had to work far away from home and came home only for weekends. When that happened, I always tried to bring something for Yehuda a rattle, a plastic duck for bathing, something like that.

One Friday afternoon, I found a very nice plastic tumbler soldier in a toyshop near the bus-station. A tumbler (in case you don't know!) is a roly-poly doll with a weight in its bottom that makes it stand up when you try laying it down. This soldier was of one piece, without any corners that could harm a baby, not too thick or too big for his hands but too big to put in his mouth. It had a black helmet, pink face, black eyes and a black twirled moustache. It was dressed in a white shirt, red vest, and green coat and held his silver sword on his shoulder, ready for fight; in one word, a picture of a hero (you can see it on the front cover of this book). We came home, my soldier and I, and fortunately I presented it first to Annie, who got alarmed: perhaps the weight in its bottom is of lead; perhaps the baby can lick off the paint. So, in her hands, my hero underwent every kind of torture. It was washed, scrubbed with soap and brush, rinsed ten times and withstood it with flying colours like the hero he was, meaning that all the colours remained as they were.

I went to the bed of the child who greeted me as always with a smile, and I put the soldier near his right hand. He touched it with a careful finger and the doll moved. The boy's face got serious. He touched it once again and the soldier wavered from side to side. Uncertain, the child recoiled and the corners of his mouth turned down, and I could already see his protecting mother throwing us both out, my soldier and me. But no. The boy took heart and put his hand on the soldier, which lay down obediently; he took his hand away and the soldier did his part and stood up. The child began to smile and Annie relaxed too. The smile got broader. Annie and I looked at our son, who pushed the tumbler firmly down and suddenly took his hand away. The tumbler sprang up at once. Yehuda began to laugh with the joy of a healthy child, free of worries, and his laughter grew stronger every time the tumbler sprang up. His laughter and careless, confident mirth made us forget the mourning and the sorrow; we put aside our worries and, like a warm spring wind, he made the ice in our souls melt, and made the memories of past sufferings fly away, and filled the room and our hearts with joy and hope.

And if fate is kind to me, the sound of that laughter I want to hear when I die.

***

Now, as experienced parents, we were no longer afraid that the old memories would disturb our children's dreams, and suddenly the years began to fly. Children I said, because in 1953 our daughter, Esther, was born. Little Esther was, even as a baby, a lively and playful child. She was not more than one year old when she raised her small arms and began to run, but she had trouble with the brakes and it was difficult for her to stop. There are those who say that, even today, she still has this problem. Yehuda was always not only the older, but also the calmer and more deliberate child. Esther, even as a girl, was impish and full of mischief until Yehuda went to the Army but, even then, she made him lose his accustomed patience by her tickling him and pulling his hair. He only got some respect from her when he was in the officer's academy. But they were good and loved each other, achieved good grades in school, and made us happy and proud.

In the background of our quiet life there was the always-threatened existence of our small country. The one-month yearly reserve service in the army, although not in the front line units because of the trouble with my ears I brought with me from the camps, was nevertheless difficult, uncomfortable and unpleasant enough. The news every hour and the recurring terror acts were a steady background and an integral part of our life. We moved from our one room apartment to a bigger one a day before the Sinai Campaign in 1956.

In 1961 I was transferred from the Jewish National Fund to a governmental office with a promotion and a higher pay, and with the possibility to leave in the course of a year with double severance pay. From hard and demanding work in the field which I did with pride and a feeling of mission, under people that demanded much from you but more from themselves, I fell into a very comfortable, but grey job, of a civil servant, mostly in the office and I felt terribly bored, and, since the end of the probation year was near, I said good-bye without fear or regret, took the severance pay and became self-employed.

The first half year was not easy but after that I began to know people, and they got to know me. I bought myself an ancient jeep, which was one of the first cars in our neighbourhood. The children were very happy and proud, and there is no reason to deny that I felt like the king of the world. Since then I have had a few cars, even new ones, but I can't forget the feeling of pride and satisfaction from that jeep, which even taught me a lesson for life. I observed that as long as it ran, it was OK, but the moment I sent it to a garage, they repaired one thing and damaged two. Since then I try to avoid doctors and physicians.

In May 1967. Nasser of Egypt expelled the UN Peacekeeping Forces from Sinai and closed the Straits of Tiran, thereby closing the Port of Eilat and threatening our borders. The Syrians and Jordan accompanied this sabre-rattling too. The shadow of the Holocaust and the invitations from anxious relatives, made us very tense, and we were wondering, what our leaders were waiting for?

5 June 1967. I had been in reserve service for more than a week in an anti-aircraft unit but had a very urgent job to do on the Lebanese border and got a day off. An army jeep found us surveying between two border stones and gazed at us dumbfounded. 'What are you doing, idiots? It has begun!' We did not ask what had begun, but ran back to my unit where they more or less knew, what in two days circled the world, namely that in the first two hours of the Six Day War, Israel had destroyed the air forces of Egypt, Syria, Iraq and Jordan. After two days it was apparent that there was no urgent need for our anti-aircraft unit and they dispersed us.

We did not dare to believe the newspapers: the way to Eilat was open; we were at the Suez Canal and in the old city of Jerusalem. Having slipped in as a journalist, I was there on the day when the new Military Governor of the Occupied Territories, General Haim Herzog, accepted the surrender and the keys of the city from the Arab notables in the Intercontinental Hotel. They did not kick me out because in those days we all floated in the air, half a metre above the earth, with an idiotic smile on our faces that took a long time to wipe off, but wipe off they did. And how!

Because they did not kick me out, I went for a short walk in the old city of Jerusalem where you could hear yet the occasional shots being fired, and see the captured Jordanian soldiers in their underwear being led to the prisoners of war camps for investigation. I stooped before a broken tobacco shop window to put back a pipe, and held it for a moment admiring it when a parachutist ran by and said to me in a reproaching tone, 'I see that you found the pipe you left here two thousand years ago. The Wailing Wall is to your right.' Well, first of all, as I said, I only wanted to put the damned pipe back in the window; and second, I had no idea that I wanted to go to the Wailing, or any other, Wall. The big, open space did not exist yet and only a narrow street led to the Wall.

I am not a religious person and I am a proud freethinker. But, even if I were religious – and this has to be said with Talmudic intonation and with the characteristic movement of the right thumb – I would strictly be against the veneration of stones, trees, graves and walls or Wall, which in my eyes is alien to religion because the God of the Jews does not need holy places. In one word, I held the Wall, kissed the warm stones and, for the first time, I wept with tears. I mourned my family, the Jewish people, wept for myself and for those like me.

I prayed the Kadish for the souls of my parents and relatives for the first time, and every time I am in Jerusalem, I go to the Wall and say Kadish.

Yehuda finished school, was conscripted and volunteered to one of the prestigious and dangerous units, but we hoped that now, after the Six Day War, there would be calmer days. No such luck. Nasser did not want to negotiate and neither did the other Arab states.

The acts of terror and the attacks on the borders were again daily occurrences and with them the retaliations in which Yehuda's unit took part, as did the officer's academy, where he trained later. So we did not have many nights without worry but he finished the three years of military service without getting hurt and began to study at the Technion. In the meantime, our Esther got called up too and she went to a new settlement in Sinai.

But luckily, Yehuda was demobilized safe and sound, unlike so many others and there are not enough words to thank for that. Yehuda finished the Technion, got his diploma as an engineer and married his girlfriend Dorit, who got her diploma at the same time.

Our daughter, Esther, was demobilized too and went back to

the kibbutz where she married her boyfriend Ron in a moving wedding ceremony together with three other couples and with the participation of the whole world and its wife.

The news of the birth of our first grandchild, Gilly, the daughter of Yehuda and Dorit, caught us in the middle of our first visit to London. Of course, the new grandmother, Annie, had no patience to finish our visit there as planned, so we came home three days earlier, and I don't let our Gilly forget that she owes us three days in London.

After the first grandchild, the ice was broken and after some months even Esther in Kibbutz Eyal - with some help from Ron - gave us a grandson, Nadav. That was very lucky, because in the meantime Yehuda got a job building highways in Kenya and took Gilly with him, but now, with Nadav, we had at least one grandchild in the neighbourhood. Our beloved Doron – a boy – was born in Kenya – and named Doron Gazit, because, as I have forgotten to mention, Yehuda changed his name to Gazit while he was in the officer's academy.

Esther and Ron, not to be outdone, gave birth to Efrat, a nice baby girl, with huge blue eyes whose nickname in the kibbutz is, 'the eyes of the country'.

After some ten years we got another nice surprise from the Gazit family: Roni, a baby girl who, of course, is the most pampered by one and all.

In 2002 I hired a bus and the whole family went on a two-week 'shorashim' trip, which in Hebrew means seeking the roots, to the places where Annie and I were born.

We travelled to Hungary and visited the village of Balkany, which was Annie's birthplace. We also visited Kassa, now Slovakia, where I was born and where my late family lived for a hundred and fifty years. We made trips to the Tatra Mountains, the Lake of Balaton and visited Budapest for some days.

You have to agree that after looking at the photo in the image section of this book that it is a nice family, touch wood! Let fate be kind to them all and bless them with health, wealth, love, happiness and a long and happy life, loved by all and loving each other.

The Americans have a nice holiday, called Thanksgiving Day. During dinner everybody has to stand up and count the blessings he has to thank God for. I give thanks for my wife, Annie, her love and inexhaustible strength, for the fact that we have now been together for some sixty years, that we are both more or less healthy for our age, for our children and grandchildren and for their love, for our life without major worries, that we have no material fears for tomorrow and for our small daily pleasures.

Let's finish this part with the most Israeli of all prayers: 'May it be not worse for us, for our family, for our relatives and friends, and may it be much, much better, for our people and our country'.

Past and Future

I have some words to say about this book, but first of all, an apology and 'proper disclosure' about the person I call Fröken Ulle, and whose name I changed, as I did all names. I fear, that her words at the end of the book present her as an unfeeling and tactless women: 'How lucky are those, who survived all that, now they have something to talk about their whole life.'

What is portrayed within those words does not do justice to how Fröken Ulle really was. You have to understand, Swedes have a real problem in finding a subject to talk about, even between friends, this is because of their reticent nature. What she meant was, that we the survivors, should never have this problem, and how right she was.

I have to explain about Sweden and Swedes too. I was there in the years of 1945-1949, nearly sixty years ago. In that time many things changed in the word, and it stands to reason that these changes were not for the better. What did not change is the gratefulness those Jews whom they saved in and after the war owe them.

Why did I write this book? Our generation stands before closing of the gates. The Americans say, that the most effective way to concentrate one's thoughts is the knowledge that you are to be hanged by daylight tomorrow. Even if there is no such dramatic occurrence awaiting me tomorrow, it is clear that I have not much time left. That is why, we, the survivors of the Holocaust are in the throws of writing. Burning in us the irrepressible compulsion to tell, to give account, to warn, to remind and to mourn a destroyed generation.

On Passover night we sing a song, a song that says that in every generation they want to destroy us, but God delivers us from their hands. Even as a child, I said how much simpler our history and His work would be if, instead of saving us from their hands, He would not let us fall into their hands in the first place.

In spite of this excellent advice of mine, fact is, that ever since becoming a nation, we always find Us in the middle of disputes between Great Powers.

We stood in the way of Babylon and they destroyed our first Temple and took us to captivity for seventy years, where we wrote the first Talmud in our boredom and took, somehow, the best jobs, so they took us back. We built the second Temple, had some troubles with the Greeks. We stood in the way of the Roman Empire, so they destroyed the second Temple and we got dispersed in the Diaspora.

They drove us out from cities and countries. At the beginnings of the Crusade, we were the first that were slaughtered; at the twelfth century they drove us out in Germany; from England in the fourteenth century; from Spain, where we were at that time proud Spanish patriots of Mosaic faith, in the forefront of culture and finances, they drove us out in the fifteenth century.

Catholics and Protestants killed each other with gusto for many years, but preferred to kill us first. The Cossacks of Bogdan Chmelnicky rebelled against Poland, but killed the Jews in hundred of thousands and, their enemies, the Poles did their best too. In the Bolshevik revolution, Jews were persecuted as capitalists, and the Ukrainian Semjon Petyura killed tens of thousands of Jews, because there were many Jews in Bolshevik leadership.

After WWI, that the Germans shamefully lost, they were full of bitterness and looked for a scapegoat, and they had not to look far. The Jews had much experience in that role. They, on their part, saw themselves as true Germans of Mosaic faith, played a leading role in culture, communication, medicine and science. In spite of the quick growth on the Nazis and the popularity of Hitler, they saw it as inconceivable that they should be in any way harmed by their beloved Homeland. It was unimaginable, just as it was in Spain of Ferdinand and Isabelle, or, of course, in

Hungary of the regent Horthy. It was unimaginable, but it happened.

The Holocaust, the tragedy of European Jews, was the expectable continuation of the history of the Jews in not to be foreseen dimensions. It was a tragic meeting at that point of the history between the ideal victim – the defenseless, homeless Jew, and the ideal murderer, the conscienceless, disciplined German Nazi. In spite of its horror and dimension, it was only the last link – up till today – of that chain and martyrdom of the homeless Jews.

The frightening thing is, the parallel between the first years of the Nazism and what happens today. The Nazis presented the Jews, as the cause of their defeat in the First World War, as the cause of their conflict of the democratic world and later as the cause of the Second World War.

The world today is marching toward a new conflict, between the Western world on one side and between the Islamic militants, mesmerized by religious ecstasy, and drunken by blood, death and fighting slogans on the other. The Muslim militants have learned the patent of the Nazis and use Israel and the Jews as a pretext, as they say the real cause of the conflict. Like Hitler's propaganda seventy years ago, that maintained that the Second World War was started at the instigations of the Jews, who made the rest of the world unite against the German fantasy of domination of the world, so with a satanic parallel, the propaganda of the militant Muslims says, that the conflict with the Western world is not because of the fact that they want to plant the black flag of their religious fanaticism on the palaces and churches of America and Europe, but because of the Jewish influence in the United States.

America and Europe are undergoing change, but as the contest and the thirst for oil grows, so the voices about the rightness of supporting Israel becomes stronger amongst the Muslim militants. You even hear queries about the prominent role the Jews play in everything. These voices are few as yet and half ashamed, because of the Holocaust, but they get louder. Of course it is wholly unimaginable that American citizens of Mosaic faith should in any way be discriminated against because of a few such, as yet subdued, voices. Yes, one remembers Spain, and Germany, and Hungary. But America? You can't compare it at all.

In the last years, the voices denying the Holocaust, and wanting to wipe Israel off the map – these two always come together – are less ashamed and are voiced not by hooligans, half mad with hate, but by a legitimate leader of a big country, with plenty of oil, Ahmedinjad of Iran, who like his illustrious predecessor, Hitler did in his time, does it in preparation of a war. Hatemongering against the Jews is a proven tool to get support from many directions. Let's not make the mistake, I don't mean that it is a pretext of any kind. They really want to destroy us, with all their heart. The exact words of Ahmedinjad: 'wipe Israel off the map.'

That is the time to tell the world, the enemies and friends from far and near: there won't be a one-sided Holocaust again. There is no future for Jews in the world without Israel, and there won't be any future for this region either without Israel. If there are people, who believe that there is another way than to cleave to this land at any price, let them think about what happened over sixty years ago: the trains rolling in the night, with their terrible load, without arousing any attention, protest or compassion. Let's all think about the millions, who were murdered, not as saints, not defending anything, but only because others wanted their annihilation, and there was nobody to save them, nobody wanting to save them.

Let's think about them with impotent rage, with clenched fist and endless sorrow.

And let's say: N e v e r   A g a i n !

Tombstones

These were the people in my family, whose names I am able to remember:

Feuerstein Etelka (Esther), Mother	1897-1944 Auschwitz
Feuerstein Miklos (Mordechai), Father	1896-1944 Auschwitz
Feuerstein Lajos, Grandfather	1864-1944 Auschwitz
Feuerstein Adel, Grandmother	1876-1944 Auschwitz
Goldberg Aliz, Aunt	1895-1944 Auschwitz
Goldberg Berti, Uncle	1890-1944 Auschwitz
Feuerstein Arpad, Uncle	1897-1942 Shot in Poland
Feuerstein Jolan, Aunt	1900-1942 Shot in Poland
Feuerstein Adel, Cousin	1936-1942 Shot in Poland
Feuerstein Rozsi, Cousin	1938-1942 Shot in Poland
Feuerstein Judit, Cousin	1939-1942 Shot in Poland
Feuerstein Emanuel, Uncle	1898-1942 Labour Service
Schapira Manyi, Aunt	1907-1944 Auschwitz
Schapira Henrik, Uncle	1902-1943 Labour Service
Schapira Juditka, Cousin	1938-1944 Auschwitz
Feuerstein Rudi, Uncle	1900-1939 Shot in Prague
Altman Magda (Dusika), Cousin	1916-1942 Auschwitz
Krauss Dora, Aunt	1878-1942 The Ghetto
Krauss Armin, Uncle	1874-1942 Auschwitz
Krauss Lajcsi, Cousin	1899-1944 Auschwitz
Krauss Jolan, Cousin	1904-1944 Auschwitz
Krauss Juditka, Cousin	1933-1944 Auschwitz
Krauss Philip, Cousin	1899-1944 Auschwitz
Krauss Iren, Cousin	1905-1944 Auschwitz
Krauss Kato, Cousin	1944-1944 Auschwitz
Licht Zsina, Aunt	1882-1942 Shot in Poland
Licht Philip, Uncle	1881-1942 Shot in Poland
Licht Ancsi, Cousin	1915-1942 Auschwitz
Licht Lili, Cousin	1919-1942 Auschwitz
Breitner Bandi, Cousin	1910-1943 Labour Service

THE TUMBLER

Altmann Anci, Cousin	1915-1943 Labour Service
Altmann Zoli, Cousin	1917-1943 Labour Service
Altmann Laci, Cousin	1920-1944 Labour Service
Altmann Desider, Uncle	1886-1943 Auschwitz
Altmann Iren, Aunt	1897-1943 Auschwitz
Altmann Boby, Cousin	1922-1945 Hanged partisan
Altmann Zoltan, Uncle	1888-1944 Auschwitz
Altmann Izso, Cousin	1922-1944 Labour Service
Baumel Lenke, Aunt	1900-1942 Shot in Poland
Boehm Elek, Uncle	1896-1944 Auschwitz
Boehm Fanny, Aunt	1896-1944 Auschwitz
Boehm Zsuzsa, Cousin	1928-1944 Auschwitz

Now some names of neighbours and classmates, of whom I don't know more than their names:

- Kis Arnold, his wife and her sister and twelve-year-old son (neighbours)
- The Breitbar Family: father, mother, their married daughter - died in Auschwitz and the daughter's husband in the Labour Service (neighbours)
- Wieder Pula, widow, and twelve-year-old daughter (neighbours)
- The Abrahamovits Family: father, mother and eleven-year-old Bumi - shot in 1939 in Kamenets Podolsk (neighbours)
- Kertesz Mano and his wife (had a neighbouring shop)

The names of some of my classmates that I can remember, all sixteen year olds like me and were sent to Auschwitz with their families in 1944:

Fischer Gyuri (Pista), Gelmann Zoli, Erdelyi Feri, Gutmann Gyuri, Preiss Tomi, Zinner Gyuri, Kardos Barna, Zipser Zoltan, Friedmann Fredi, Friedmann Imre.

There were nine more in our class, but I am unable to recall their names, and there were so many, many more.
May they not be forgotten!

Related website: www.anti-semite.com

Acknowledgments

Heartfelt thanks to all my cousins and, first of all, to Haim Krauss in Kibbutz Kfar Masaryk, for their help in gathering the material about our relatives, the Altmanns, in Eperjes (Presov).

Thanks to Pamela Segev for her work in editing this book (pre-publisher), for her patience and for making it more fit for human consumption.

Thanks to Raanan Beeri, graphic artist and second cousin, for designing the front cover of this book and for his patience.

To Elimelech Barak for his help in designing *The Tumbler* (pre-publisher).

To Ron Kohen-Perrera from Kibbutz Kfar Masaryk for his help with the pictures.

THE TUMBLER

Other Titles by this Publisher

*Burnt: Surviving Against all the Odds – Beaten, Burnt and Left for
Dead. One Man's Inspiring Story of His Survival After Losing His Legs*
Ian Colquhoun
Cosmic Ordering Connection
Stephen Richards
Cosmic Ordering Guide
Stephen Richards
Cosmic Ordering Healing Oracle Cards
Stephen Richards
Cosmic Ordering: Oracle Wish Cards
Stephen Richards & Karen Whitelaw Smith
Cosmic Ordering Service: 101 Orders For Daily Use
Stephen Richards
The Butterfly Experience: Inspiration For Change
Karen Whitelaw Smith
Past Life Tourism
Barbara Ford-Hammond
*The Real Office: An Uncharacteristic Gesture of Magnanimity
by Management Supremo Hilary Wilson-Savage*
Hilary Wilson-Savage

Prospective Titles
*Cosmic Ordering - Chakra Clearing for a Better
Connection: Oracle Cards*
Stephen Richards
Life Without Lottie
Fiona Fridd
Mrs Darley's Pagan Whispers
Carole Carlton
Occult: The Psychic Jungle
Jonathan Charles Tapsell

Mirage Publishing Website:
www.miragepublishing.com

Submissions of Mind, Body & Spirit manuscripts
welcomed from new authors.